D1563916

Revolution and Political Instability

Revolution and Political Instability

Applied Research Methods

Stephen J. Andriole
International Information Systems, Inc.
and
Gerald W. Hopple
Defense Systems, Inc.

St. Martin's Press, New York

Library of Congress Cataloging in Publication Data

Andriole, Stephen J.
   Revolution and political instability.

   Bibliography: p.
   Includes indexes.
   1. Political stability—Research.   2. Revolutions—
Research.   I. Hopple, Gerald W.   II. Title.
JC330.2.A52 1984   321.09'072   83–40704
ISBN 0–312–67991–2

Figures 2.4 and 2.5 both appeared in J. A. Goldstone, 'Theories of Revolution: The Third Generation,' *World Politics* **32** (April 1980), pp. 425–53, and are reprinted with permission.

Figures 2.2 and 3.4 originally appeared in Charles Tilly, *From Mobilization to Revolution* (Addison-Wesley, 1978), and are reprinted with permission.

Contents

List of Figures

List of Tables

Preface

This book is the result of several different research projects. It is the result of work that we conducted into the nature and purpose of analytical methodology. It is the result of research that we jointly pursued in political instability and, to a certain extent, it represents a continuation of some research in 'policy relevance' that we began over a decade ago. The book is thus the product of a lot of diverse effort which stretches over a very long period of time.

We wrote the book in order to do at least three things. First, we wanted to survey the qualitative and quantitative research in revolution and political instability that had been published since around 1960. Second, we wanted to describe the research in some ways that made sense to those who either had to build upon it or actually use it and, finally, we wanted to render an assessment of its applied utility.

The book's intended audience includes all those who must describe, explain, or predict revolution and political instability. The most obvious consumers are those in the government or industry directly responsible for such tasks. It is interesting that industry now recognizes an 'intelligence' function, a function that, of course, governments have long since held very dear to their operations. Hence, the reader will find frequent references to intelligence and intelligence analysis throughout the book. But please remember that our use of the terms is generic, applying to all those who must produce and implement intelligence.

We of course owe a number of debts to those who helped us prepare the book. Denise M. Andriole prepared the original manuscript. John Correnti, Ed Bilheimer, and Phyllis Hutchinson prepared the illustrations and figures, while general support was obtained from both International Information Systems, Inc. and Defense Systems, Inc. We would also like to acknowledge the anonymous reviews of several individuals who made the book more readable than it was when it first came out of the typewriter. In spite of all this help, we alone are responsible for the problems in the book that no doubt still remain. While we have tried to find and solve them all, no doubt some slipped by. Hopefully, they are of little real consequence.

SJA and GWH
April 1984

Part I
Introduction

1 Introduction

The backdrop

In virtually every part of the world today we can find regimes that are far from stable. Coups, riots, and revolutions occur on what seems to be an almost regular basis in the Third World. Few societies are free from mass protest or intense political conflict. Yet while many nations behave the same, they are analytically distinct. In fact, one can argue that each potential regime change or collapse presents a set of unique analytical and national problems.

Given the pervasiveness and importance of political instability and the uniqueness of each case, the need for systematic analysis has never been greater. But how can we ensure the production of the best possible analyses and estimates? We see at least three steps. The first involves surveying the political instability research terrain in order to find out what has already been done. The second involves categorizing it according to some meaningful applied analytical criteria, and the third involves assessing just how useful it might be to the analyst faced with an impossible deadline and a difficult-to-please superior.

This book attempts to do these three things. Hopefully, its contents will contribute to the process of analysis and estimates.

Problems

Basic and applied quantitative and qualitative research on foreign political instability has proceeded from so many different perspectives that research cumulation has been much slower than desirable. For example, for years so-called 'traditional' or qualitative analysts have attempted to describe, explain, and predict political instability via the adoption of economic, historical, and institutional approaches. Simultaneously, quantitative analysts have developed computer models, data bases, and 'indicators' of political instability. The analysts themselves have backgrounds in history, economics, political science, sociology, operations research, engineering, systems analysis, comparative politics, and computer science, among other formal disciplines and informal fields of inquiry. Consequently, qualitative and quantitative research findings have not by and large been publicized through any common professional society, journal, or publisher. Moreover, since much of the research has been conducted outside of academia, it has seldom been evaluated against its more widely distributed counterpart.

The diversity in methodological perspective, background, training, experience, and distribution practices of political instability researchers continues to contribute directly to the lack of research cumulation in political instability. The diversity also contributes to a communications gap among those interested in describing, explaining, and predicting political instability. The simple truth is that different research groups speak very different technical languages. Those who need to assimilate this diverse research must thus translate the research findings into language useful for their purposes, or forgo the benefit of an integrated and balanced picture.

Yet another problem directly related to the diversity of past and ongoing political instability research is the infrequency with which methodological evaluations have been undertaken. It is thus difficult to assess how effective individual methods and techniques have been in the past or are likely to be in the future; methodological investment decisions are especially difficult to make when such assessments cannot be made.

Objectives

This book deals with the three problems described above. It identifies and categorizes the diverse methodological research which has been conducted over the past twenty years and assesses its applied utility to intelligence analysis. The book also attempts to bridge the communications gap between producers and consumers of research into political instability by translating the jargon which pervades the study of political instability into language understandable to the widest possible audience.

Part II of this book examines a great deal of the research into political instability conducted in academia, industry, and government since 1960. The purpose of this section is to identify the qualitative and quantitative descriptive, explanatory, and predictive research that has been published in report, article, monograph and book form during the past twenty years. Part II is also designed to assess how successful or unsuccessful the research has been from an analytical perspective. Part III turns to applied effectiveness. Given the analytical results discovered in Part II, how likely are they—and the methods which led to them—to help intelligence analysts monitor, explain, and predict foreign political processes? Are they only useful for the conduct of basic research and the eventual development of theory? A number of evaluative criteria are developed in Part III to help answer these and other questions, criteria based upon an assessment of what it is intelligence analysts need and want to do. Part III concludes the book with a set of assessments regarding what to read, encourage, and invest in; it also outlines the conditions and circumstances under which some methods can be used productively and some should be avoided. A single Appendix contains a glossary of many of the most commonly used terms, concepts, and methods connected with the analysis of political instability. Finally, a subject and author index is included for quick reference purposes.

Part II
Political instability research, 1960–1983

2 Qualitative Political Instability Analysis

History has been almost a continuous stream of change, up-heaval, and violence. Conflict and cooperation continue to be as central to politics within nations as they are to relations between nations. Internal political conflict may be (and often is) non-violent and 'routine.' But just as international conflict is often a continuation of politics by other means, so too do violence and revolution often proceed from 'normal' domestic political processes (Aya, 1979).

Political and social philosophers have expressed an enduring concern with 'political instability.' The major classical theorists include Aristotle, Hobbes, de Tocqueville, Marx, and Durkheim. Unfortunately, a systematic review and evaluation of political and social thought about revolution and instability in its many forms is beyond the scope of this book; our primary concern is with the *application* of various methods, approaches, and techniques to political instability analysis. However, most of the classical theorists are reflected in the work of one or more current students. Tilly (1978), for example, does a very good job of tracing current theories of political violence and revolution to Marx, John Stuart Mill, Emile Durkheim, and Max Weber.

The perennial 'what,' 'why,' and 'when' questions that intrigued the classical theorists, and continue to fascinate and bewilder contemporary ones, are used here to launch our survey. Some of them include the following:

— What is political instability?
— What are the major types of instability?
— What are the patterns of instability in countries and across time?
— Why does it occur?
— What are the long-term and short-term preconditions for

instability and what are the immediate catalysts or precipitants?
— Does it flow from a 'state of mind' within a population, from forces within a society or polity, or from the state of society itself?
— Are there determinants beyond the borders of a country?
— Is political instability 'normal' or 'abnormal'?
— Is it random or deterministic?
— To paraphrase the central theme of Eckstein's (1980) assessment of two competing approaches to the subject, is political instability an inherent feature of political life (the outgrowth of normal routines and political processes, something that is not only possible but probable), or is it something rare and contingent (admittedly possible but not very probable)?
— What about the processes by which political instability unfolds and ends? How do we get from cause to outcome and consequence?
— Can we forecast political instability? Are there indicators or 'signals'? Or, is instability unpredictable?

Our survey is organized around these questions and the related goals of description, explanation, and prediction. We have divided the research into the qualitative and the quantitative, thus generating a matrix formed by the intersection of two generic methods and three analytical foci, as suggested in Figure 2.1.

For the purposes of this book, descriptive research includes

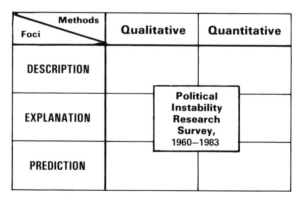

Methods / Foci	Qualitative	Quantitative
DESCRIPTION		
EXPLANATION	Political Instability Research Survey, 1960–1983	
PREDICTION		

Fig. 2.1   Survey Organization

research that focuses on the intranational and international factors that contribute to political instability. Detailed analyses of specific factors, such as labor unrest, shortages, and repression, and individual country case studies, are included in the review of descriptive political instability research. Explanatory research includes those studies and analyses that attempt to explain why political instability occurs generally and in specific geographical regions and countries. It also includes research attempts to link the characteristics of certain economic and political systems to the occurrence of political instability. Predictive research attempts to correlate factors like economic scarcity, political repression, and ethnic conflict and, based upon systematic extrapolations, determine the likelihood of future political instability. Much of this research has focused upon the likelihood of political instability in specific countries, but a lot of it has also stressed the prediction of conditions likely to trigger political instability regardless of geographical region or recent political history. Those who attempt to predict political instability on a case-by-case basis usually believe that predictions are inherently grounded in the particular events and conditions of individual societies, while those who attempt to predict instability generally often believe that certain events trigger instability regardless of where or in what countries the events occur.

Qualitative research usually involves the use of methods and approaches which rely principally upon the wisdom, experience, and judgment of the researcher. Qualitative researchers frequently adopt historical, institutional, and sociological approaches within single and comparative case study analyses. Contrary to some views of methodology, qualitative researchers frequently use quantitative concepts and data. But they do not use them in the same way as quantitative researchers, who use 'hard' data to test hypotheses about political instability. More to the point, quantitative researchers frequently attempt to apply the 'scientific method' to the study of political instability. For example, concepts like political repression would be converted by the quantitative researcher into data (representing, perhaps, the number of government crackdowns or number of government censors) and then used to test a specific hypothesis about political instability, such as one which states that as the level of political repression rises over time so does the likelihood of instability (which would also have to be defined precisely). If successful, the quantitative researcher can state that a relationship exists between repression and instability and that for every unit increase in repression one can expect a unit increase in the likelihood of instability.

In the last two decades, hundreds of quantitative studies have appeared which try to profile, explain, and (less frequently) forecast the trends, patterns, and processes of political instability. Long books are now needed just to summarize the literature and guide us through endless charts, tables, equations, symbols, hypotheses, conclusions, qualifications, and quarrels. In contrast, people have studied instability *qualitatively* for more than the last two millennia. Below we present an abbreviated tour of the qualitative landscape— a blurry snapshot overview rather than a full-length technicolor movie.

Qualitative description

Qualitative descriptive research into political instability has by and large focused on the following areas:

— case studies of political instability and revolutions;
— definitions of political instability—usually grounded in definitions of collective action;
— classifications of political instability;
— typologies of political instability and revolutions; and
— stages through which revolutions can be expected to pass.

Goldstone (1980) sees early qualitative descriptive work as *ad hoc* and implicit. Empirical reality was typically injected into case studies by way of 'illustrative cases' rather than systematic evidence, analysis, and comparison. Consequently, researchers often 'ransacked' history for supporting cases and ignored or explained away cases that contradicted, qualified, or negated their arguments. *The emphasis was on minute description, leading to the application of the label of 'natural history' as a catch-all term for the entire analytical genre.*

Beyond the analysis of isolated cases, qualitative descriptive research has also yielded discussions about what political instability is, how to classify it, and how to identify the various stages of revolution. Definitions of political instability naturally always include definitions of politics. We know from Lasswell (1936), for example, that politics is the 'study of influence and the influential,' the study of elites and their beliefs and actions. But even if elites are at center stage, there is still a 'mass,' or non-elite, audience. Students of mass or collective action, who study history from the bottom up and whose work is exemplified by Charles Tilly, do not subscribe to the Lasswellian dictum, which, interestingly, even Lasswell modified in his monumental *Politics: Who Gets What, When, How* in the 1930s.

Tilly's (1975, 1978, 1983) work on collective action provides a useful point of departure for attempting to *define political instability*. His theory of collective action is neither intrinsically qualitative nor quantitative and in fact is often based on statistical data. What does mark the theory is its blending of sound sociology with verifiable history. Tilly's model of collective action (CA)—also known as the resource mobilization (RM) approach—consists of five elements:

— interests of actors;
— organization (which most directly affects the capacity of a group of actors to act in its own interest);
— mobilization (the process of acquiring collective control over necessary resources);
— opportunity (the relationship between the group and the world around it); and
— collective action (which results from changing combinations of interests, organizations, mobilization, and opportunity.

Tilly's CA theory is based on Marx–plus. Marx highlighted the key role of major classes and their interests—which emerge from the organization of production—whereas Tilly expands this notion to include generally shared interests. He also adds Max Weber and, especially, John Stuart Mill, to the picture. For Weber, interests lead to beliefs, which in turn lead to organization (for example, social movements) and CA. In routine situations (outside the domain of instability), interests and beliefs are interrelated: beliefs determine organization and interests determine CA. In non-routine situations (which we refer to as 'instability'), interests lead to beliefs, beliefs shape organizations and CA, and organization leads to CA. Figure 2.2

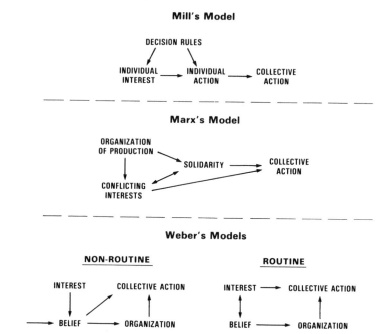

(From Tilly, 1978)

Fig. 2.2 Mill's, Marx's, and Weber's Models of Collective Action

shows Weber's models, depicting and therefore clarifying the cluttered verbal material necessary to discuss the ideas. Also shown are the models of Marx and Mill, who maintained that CA is a function of the pursuit of individual interests.

According to many qualitative analysts, instability flows out of CA, which is a continuum ranging from dormant to peaceful to violent. Most collective violence, as Tilly (1975, 1978) points out, however, is an outgrowth of actions which were not initially or intrinsically violent and is often brought about by agents of the state, not by mobilized collective actors. *Revolution, according to this viewpoint, is an extreme (but not qualitatively different) condition of the normal political process. It is not, therefore, as Crane Brinton (1938) contended, a disease or fever which erupts outside the bounds of normal politics.*

Political violence is defined by Tilly (1975, 1978) as

interaction that leads to the seizure or damage of persons or objects, so long as resistance occurs. But this definition skirts a consideration of intentions and outcomes; it also restricts the scope of instability to collective or mass action. Elite repression, elite conspiracies, and coups are therefore not part of Tilly's definition. But we know that elite activity is often related to mass violence. Elite repression may precede or follow collective violence; elite conspiracies may (or may not) be linked to violent CA; and elite *coups d'état* may also be associated with the occurrence of political instability.

Qualitative descriptive research has also included *classifications of political instability*. Again, Tilly (1975, 1978) provides our example.[1] He distinguished between communal and associational types of collective action, thereby excluding random or spontaneous activity. Associational groups are relatively formal, organized, 'rational,' and modern. Contending groups within a nation may be those which are trying to get into the system (challengers), those which are already in and are competing for resources and power, and those which are on the way out and are losing power. *Tilly argues that 'random' or spontaneous instability is rare or non-existent.* We disagree. While there is extensive evidence of collective protest in all types of societies (Zimmermann 1980), there is no really convincing evidence that such protest is always organized, at least in the same sense that group-based CA is. We have therefore modified Tilly's typology in Figure 2.3 to include an initial branch for spontaneous versus organized activity; the right side of the figure depicts Tilly's communal/associational group types and the challenging/competitive/losing power categories, while the left recognizes the possibility of spontaneous violence.

Many quantitative descriptive analysts have neglected general CA in favor of revolution, a highly specific, relatively rare (but undeniably important) example of CA. Some definitions of revolutions are precise and narrow (Huntington 1968; Skocpol 1979). Often, however, it has been defined less rigidly, with the inevitable efforts to classify revolutions into distinct types. One of the best-known—and most frequently cited—comes from Chalmers Johnson (1964). He uses four criteria—targets, perpetrators, goals, and initiation—to develop six kinds of revolutions.

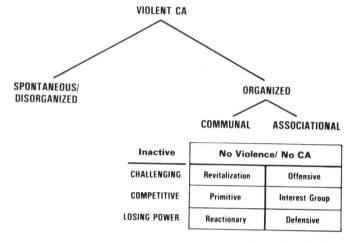

(From Tilly, 1978)

Fig. 2.3 Tilly's (Modified) Typology of Violent CA

— Jacquerie (a mass rebellion of peasants with limited goals):
  — French peasant rebellion (1358);
  — Russian peasant rebellion (1773–5).
— Millennarian rebellion (prophet-led, with the goal of creating an ideal society);
  — Taiping rebellion, China (1851–64);
  — Zapata in Mexico (1910–19);
  — Boxer rebellion in China (1899–1900).
— Anarchistic rebellion (anti-nationalistic and utopian):
  — Vendée counter-revolution, France (1793–6);
  — Tibetan rebellion (1959);
  — American Civil War (1861–5).
— Jacobin communist revolution (classic revolution, fundamental societal change):
  — French Revolution (1789–99);
  — Turkish Revolution (1908–22);
  — Mexican Revolution (1910–34);
  — Russian Revolution, Kerensky (March 1917).
— Conspiratorial *coup d'état* (elite-based, elitist goals):
  — Russian Revolution, Lenin (October 1917);
  — Irish Rebellion (1916);
  — Castro in Cuba (1959).

— Militarized mass insurrection (elite leading the masses with nationalistic goals):
  — China (1937–49);
  — Algeria (1954–62);
  — Ireland (1916–23);
  — Philippines (1946–54); and
  — Malaya (1948–58).

There are many qualitative typologies, but they are all different, and nobody likes anyone else's.[2] Skocpol (1979), for example, focuses on the French, Russian (Lenin, not Kerensky), and Chinese Revolutions, maintaining that all three are basically similar; Johnson puts them into three different categories. He also assigns Turkey's Revolution to the Jacobin communist category, a classification decision which continues to raise quite a few eyebrows, including Trimberger's (1978), who categorizes Turkey along with Japan (1869), Egypt (1952), and Peru (1968). Algeria, Vietnam, and many other Third World revolutions have also been lumped together.

Another major output of the so-called natural history school has been the *identification of sets of stages through which revolutions are supposed to pass.* David Schwartz (1968, 1972) provides a good example of this research. He articulates a process-oriented theory of political alienation, suggesting a sequence from allegiance to ambivalence, passive alienation, and active alienation. According to Schwartz, the 'typical' revolutionary situation passes through the following ten stages:

— withdrawal (initial political alienation);
— origin of revolutionary organizations;
— revolutionary appeals;
— revolutionary coalition and movement building processes;
— non-violent revolutionary politics;
— outbreak of revolutionary violence;
— rule of the moderates;
— accession of the extremists;
— reign of terror; and
— Thermidor.

In summary, it is very safe to say that virtually all of the qualitative descriptive research that has been conducted in the twentieth century has its roots in the classical theoretical work of Aristotle, Hobbes, de Tocqueville, Marx, Durkheim, Mill, and Weber. The researchers of the past two decades owe no less a debt to these classical theorists. Much of the early qualitative descriptive research on political instability evolved into what is known as the 'natural history' school of thought, which regards revolution as akin to a disorder worthy of detailed scrutiny.

Related qualitative descriptive research developed definitions of political instability. Some researchers have depicted instability as mass collective action, where mass interests are converted into attitudes and beliefs, which in turn affect organization and collective action, which can lead to political instability. Ideas traceable to Weber assign great importance to interests and organization; Marxists stress material interests; while the followers of Mill believe that political instability can result from the pursuit of individual interests.

Many qualitative political instability researchers attribute a great deal of descriptive importance to the nature of the collective action that a nation is experiencing. Violent collective action is seen by many as an extreme—but not at all pathological—condition of the normal political process, thus contradicting many of the early theorists who regarded revolution as a disease or a fever which erupts outside the bounds of normal politics.

Political violence is defined by many as a phenomenon which destroys people and property that is resisted by an alternative or competing force. The sources of political violence can be collective or elitist. Random or spontaneous violence is as possible as 'organized' violence.

Some qualitative descriptive analysts have attempted to classify revolutions according to a number of criteria, which usually include the targets, perpetrators, goals, and catalysts of revolution. But very few classifications have been accepted by the qualitative descriptive research community.

The 'natural historians' have also identified the stages through which political violence and revolutions can be expected to pass, though the stages have not been verified empirically or even through an analysis of multiple case studies.

Qualitative explanation

The qualitative explanatory political instability research discussed below focuses on the following areas:

— explanations grounded in history and sociology and frequently generated via a comparative historical approach;
— explanations attributable to the position and behavior of the agrarian, peasant, or otherwise disenfranchised classes in society;
— explanations attributable to the activity of the elites in society;
— explanations grounded in surveys of civilizations and broad social change;
— explanations attributable to national, social, and political structure, the impact of international pressures, and assumptions about national autonomy;
— explanations based upon detailed single, multiple, and comparative case studies; and
— explanations grounded in research on social movements, ethnicity, and terrorism.

Explanation is concerned with 'why' and 'how' political instability occurs, with the conditions which lead to political instability, how instability evolves, and with the consequences of instability. The qualitative explanation school is particularly compelling when it deals with precondition questions, although its practitioners under-attend to the intervening processes of instability: how a nation moves from preconditions to consequences. Many of these theories also center round revolutions, again neglecting the many kinds of violent or collective action which are less intense and dramatic but much more frequent.

The qualitative explanatory school is extremely well grounded in history and sociology. As the leading current practitioner of the comparative historical method for studying revolutions sees it (Skocpol 1979), the approach is midway between the atheoretical 'natural history' approach of Crane Brinton and the like, who often looked at only a few cases, and the quantitative social science theories, which typically analyze a lot of cases and a lot of data. *The comparative historical approach uses comparative case studies (situations where there are many influences or variables, but a limited number of actual cases) and tries to generalize across cases while remaining grounded in actual history.*

Some approaches involve the juxtaposition of sharply contrasting cases to bring out the unique features of each, some use parallel cases in support of a single theory, while still others rely on two or more cases in an effort to test broad theories about societal conditions and processes as determinants of .instability (Skocpol and Somers 1980). The different forms of historical comparison share the features of being qualitative and explanatory at the same time (although the contrasting cases approach is not always useful for developing explanations).

The Marxist theory of revolution (with amendments and additions from Lenin, Mao, Ho, Giap, and Che Guevara) is a good example of qualitative explanatory analysis. The theory, which has been studied from both basic and 'applied' perspectives, revolves around four basic ideas:

— Revolution is a class-based movement which grows out of 'objective structural' contradictions.
— The key to analyzing any society is its mode of production or combination of socio-economic forces of production (technology and the division of labor) and class relations.
— The fundamental source of the revolutionary contradiction, the gap within a mode of production between social forces and social relations of production, is expressed in increased class conflict.
— A successful revolution involves a transition from the previous mode of production and form of class dominance to a completely new mode of production, with new social relations of production and new prevailing political and ideological forms.

Tilly (1978) points out that Marxist analysis has been modified somewhat in the twentieth century, with variations in the relative weight assigned to Marx's key factors. Perhaps the key revision is the recognition that there are significant actors in addition to social classes (for example, ethnic groups and religious movements).

Nearly all of the qualitative explanatory studies since 1970 are heavily indebted to two landmark books published in the 1960s: Barrington Moore's *Social Origins of Dictatorship and Democracy* (1966) and Eric Wolf's *Peasant Wars of the Twentieth Century* (1969). Sheehan (1980) places Moore's *Social Origins* in the context of other 'classic' works. Moore argues that the nature of revolutions depends very much on the fates of agrarian classes during the processes of commercialization of agriculture and state expansion. The specific nature of the class coalition which spawns the revolution has a tremendous impact on the nature of political organization afterwards: for example, a bureaucrat–landlord combination tends to produce fascism. Moore focuses on England, France, the United States, China, Japan, and India (with attention also given to Germany and Russia).

Wolf (1969) analyzes revolutions in Mexico, Russia, China, Vietnam, Algeria, and Cuba. He focuses on the structural foundations of peasant life, discusses the impact on peasants of both national and international markets, and talks about the conditions under which peasants respond to threats with force. (All three themes pervade later work on peasants and revolution.) Wolf sees the middle peasants as the primary revolutionary actors, the level of peasantry most 'available' for revolutionary movements.

Skocpol (1982) provides an excellent review essay which discusses and critiques three of the major peasant studies: Wolf's (1969), Migdal's (1974) theory of how imperialistic, modernizing forces impinge on peasant villages, and Paige's (1975) analysis of agrarian movements from 1948–70 in 135 Third World agricultural sectors. Colburn (1982), Goldstone (1980), and Scott (1977) are all worth looking at as well. In addition, Disch (1979), Wolf (1977), and Somers and Goldfrank (1979) provide assessments of Paige (1975).

But what do we know about peasants and revolution? Unfortunately, the research leads to confusion rather than clarity. Wolf (1969) attempts to generalize inductively on the basis of six twentieth-century cases. Migdal (1974) develops a theory of how imperialistic, modernizing forces impinge on peasant villages, based on fifty-one published village studies in eighteen Asian and Latin American countries as well as his own field experience in India and Mexico. Paige (1975) undertakes a quantitative analysis of agrarian movements from 1948 to 1970 in 135 agricultural export sectors in seventy Third World countries and supplements this with in-depth accounts for Peru, Angola, and Vietnam.

Wolf (1969) sees middle peasants as the most likely participants in revolutionary movements, and Paige (1975) develops predictions on the basis of the structure of peasant/landlord relations, especially whether or not peasants and landlords get their income from land ownership, wages and capital, or diverse combinations. A mass peasant revolution is likely when landlords rely on land ownership for their income and peasants are either shareholders or migratory laborers. This particular combination is likely to lead to an agrarian revolution in which a strong peasant-based guerrilla movement organized by a nationalist or communist party tries to overthrow the rural upper class and overturn the institutions of the state, replacing them with a new society. *Migdal (1974) assigns primary responsibility for revolution to political organizations; armed revolutionary parties are the key agents who directly mobilize peasant support.*

Where Wolf singles out middle peasants and Paige landless peasants, Skocpol (1979, 1982) contends that it is not landholding that accounts for revolutionary activity, but the structure of the peasant community in its entirety, as well as relations between the landed upper class and the agrarian lower class. *According to Skocpol, relatively autonomous peasant communities are the most prone to revolutionary activity.*

Trimberger's *Revolutions from Above* moves the focus to *elite based revolutions* and attempts to explain four cases of such instability (Turkey in 1923, the Mejii Restoration in Japan in 1868, and coups in Egypt in 1952 and Peru in 1968). In all four instances, traditional rulers were ousted and extensive programs of modernization were launched. The critical determinant of these kinds of revolution is a particular type of elite structure, one in which the bureaucracy and the military perpetrators of the transformation are separated from the landlord and merchant classes. The usefulness of distinguishing between mass and elite revolutions is highlighted by the difference in outcomes. The outcomes of 'revolutions from above' are quite different from the much more thorough changes triggered by mass-based revolutionary upheaval, as Goldstone (1980: 439) notes:

. . . while the initial phases of modernization may have been successful, the unavoidable alliance of officials with local landlords, and the consequent entrenchment of those landlords, ruled out the emergence of domestic capitalist economies that were not heavily dependent on the more advanced Western economies.

Eisenstadt (1978, 1980), like Trimberger (1978), adopts the

comparative method of using parallel cases to demonstrate the applicability of a single theory. He offers what is undoubtedly the most wide-ranging and ambitious qualitative theory of revolution in his comparative survey of civilizations and social change. The concrete 'cases' go from the Chinese, Russian, and Byzantine Empires to Western Europe, ancient Greece, certain Near Eastern societies, and Buddhist, Hindu, and Islamic civilizations. His theory is also unique in the emphasis given to cultural orientations. Figure 2.4 presents Eisenstadt's approach. Imperial–feudal regimes are the most likely to experience

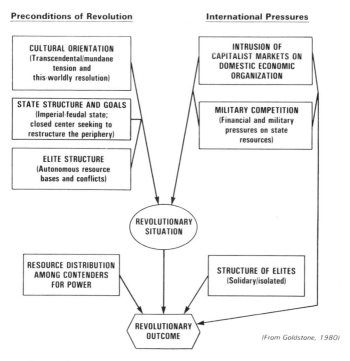

Preconditions of Revolution   **International Pressures**

CULTURAL ORIENTATION
(Transcendental/mundane tension and this-worldly resolution)

INTRUSION OF CAPITALIST MARKETS ON DOMESTIC ECONOMIC ORGANIZATION

STATE STRUCTURE AND GOALS
(Imperial-feudal state; closed center seeking to restructure the periphery)

MILITARY COMPETITION
(Financial and military pressures on state resources)

ELITE STRUCTURE
(Autonomous resource bases and conflicts)

REVOLUTIONARY SITUATION

RESOURCE DISTRIBUTION AMONG CONTENDERS FOR POWER

STRUCTURE OF ELITES
(Solidary/isolated)

REVOLUTIONARY OUTCOME   *(From Goldstone, 1980)*

Fig. 2.4 Eisenstadt's Model of Revolution

a revolution. A distinctive pattern of change characterizes such societies: changes in a variety of cultural and institutional spheres come together or coalesce. Religious heterodoxy, political rebellion, and demands for social change coincide and reinforce each other, leading to a transformation of the existing regime. This pattern of change is the primary cause of revolutions. The 'structural preconditions' (state and elite structure) and international pressures must also be present but are not enough in and of themselves to bring about revolution. Examples of such imperial–feudal regimes include Western and Central Europe, the Byzantine Empire, China, and Russia.

Eisenstadt identifies two additional contrasting categories. First, there are the societies which show the pattern of simultaneous and interrelated change processes, but with short-lived institutions (for example, Greek and other city-states of antiquity and ancient Israelite and Islamic tribal federations). Second, there are patrimonial societies, which show very few instances of changes across institutional spheres occurring together (South and South-east Asia, the ancient Near East, most Islamic societies). In such societies there was little connection between changes in political regimes and variations in the social and economic spheres.

Theda Skocpol (1979) offers a theory of revolution which is less grandiose than Eisenstadt's and much better grounded in the processes of historical change. Skocpol's theory integrates three ideas:

- a structural perspective;
- the impact of the international context and external pressures; and
- the autonomy of the state.

Figure 2.5 displays Skocpol's analytical scheme, which she applied to the revolutions in France, Russia, and China.

The structural perspective involves an adamant rejection of 'voluntarism,' the viewpoint that revolution is a process which realizes intentional human purposes. A structural interpretation emphasizes objective relationships in society and actual conflict among groups and nations. Such forces determine revolutions; people do not engineer them. Historically, Skocpol contends, no successful revolution has been *made. Revolutionary situations develop out of political-military crises of the state and patterns of class domination. The outcome of revolutions are in a sense predetermined and are neither fully foreseen nor completely intended by the participants.*

The international context introduces the impact of the internationally uneven spread of capitalist economic development. Unequal or competitive relations between states help to shape

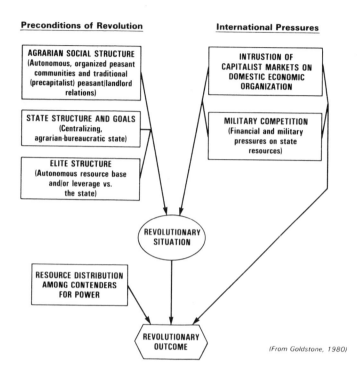

Fig. 2.5 Skocpol's Model of Revolution

a society's state and class structures, thereby affecting the domestic context from which revolution arises. *According to Skocpol, modern social revolutions have occurred only in states occupying internationally disadvantageous positions.*

Skocpol's views on the state as an autonomous player are a noteworthy departure from orthodox Marxist theorizing. According to Skocpol, the state cannot be reduced to socio-economic forces and conflicts. It is an autonomous entity that has a logic and interests all its own.

Skocpol uses the factors sketched out in Figure 2.5 to explain *social revolutions, which are defined as rapid, basic transformations of a society's state and class structures, along with the occurrence of class-based revolts from below.* The revolutions in France, Russia, and China are very similar examples of social-revolutionary transformations. (Note the lumping together of what are often regarded as the prototypical 'bourgeois' versus 'Marxist' revolutions.) All three upheavals are similar in terms of their Old Regimes and revolutionary processes and outcomes. All three revolutions occurred in wealthy and politically ambitious agrarian states which had never been colonized by another power. In all three cases, the following sequence held: externally mediated crises and internal structural conditions and trends led to the incapacitation of the central state machineries. Widespread lower class rebellion followed (especially by peasants), along with efforts by mass-mobilizing leaders to consolidate the power of a new revolutionary state.

Skocpol's scope is not restricted to the 'Big Three.' In addition to unearthing a number of similarities (as well as isolating differences) among the French, Russian, and Chinese revolutions, she contrasts them with 'negative cases.' She looks at the very different conditions, processes, and outcomes which characterized England in the 1600s (a political revolution), Prussia in the early 1800s and Japan in the 1860s (examples of Trimberger's 'revolutions from above'), Germany in 1848, and Russia in 1905 (two failed revolutions). Finally, Skocpol universalizes social revolution by noting the broad resemblances of Mexico, Algeria, Cuba, and other Third World revolutions to the Big Three. A major qualification, however, is that the Third World cases have faced two factors irrelevant to the trio: the legacies of colonialism and the much greater impact of foreign sponsors and transnational economic relations. Her work is thus a genuine comparative historical analysis. It relies on a huge set of secondary sources to compare and contrast three positive cases and some negative-contrast cases selected from the period since the end of the Renaissance with applicability up to the present.

Part I of *States and Social Revolutions* concerns the structural and historical sources of revolutionary situations, where Skocpol concentrates on three sets of factors:

— The political crises of absolutist states, with the analysis centering on:
    — monarchy/dominant class factors;
    — agrarian economy;
    — international pressures;
— Conditions for peasant insurrections in terms of:
    — agrarian class structures;
    — local politics; and

— Societal transformations:
  — with respect to the three social revolutions; and
  — for England, Prussia, and Japan.

Part II lists common patterns and differences for social revolutionary outcomes. Central to this part of her analysis is the question of how the form of the revolutionary crisis and the Old Regime legacy both shaped and limited the subsequent efforts of the state-building revolutionary elites. Also of importance was the nature and timing of peasant revolts, whether sudden and autonomous (France and Russia) or delayed (China). Peasants turned out to be uniquely influential in shaping the New Regime in China which came to power after the extended revolutionary process from 1911 to 1949. Skocpol (1979: 282-3) offers a summary of the findings about outcomes, organized around the:

— effects of social revolutionary crises;
— socio-economic legacies of Old Regimes;
— international and world-historical conditions;
— processes of revolutionary state-building; and the
— nature of new regimes.

In their review of *States and Revolutions*, Himmelstein and Kimmel (1981) correctly note that Skocpol's masterful study successfully blends de Tocqueville into a general Marxian framework. At the same time the work is a synthesis which rejects core ideas from Marx, including, and most importantly, the Marxian theory of self-conscious revolutionary movements rooted in class conflict as the primary and indispensable aspect of revolution.

Revolutions, in Skocpol's view, are not the result of contradictions between the forces and relations of production within society. Nor are revolutions the products of rising classes. Instead, revolutions reflect peasant uprisings, conflict between the state and the landed upper class (which initially sets the process in motion and leads to the first real collapse of the Old Regime, which can occur before other social elements have been mobilized), and marginal elite movements. Skocpol is also indebted to Barrington Moore (1966), Wolf (1969), and the other students of peasant revolutions. But she clearly builds beyond all of her predecessors. *The net result is a genuine theory of revolution, based on the core concepts of state and agrarian and other class structures, and transnational economic and military relations, all solidly grounded in history and comparative analysis.*

We shall defer an assessment of the analytical utility of Skocpol and other qualitative explanatory theories until Part III. At this point, however, we can note some of the problems of this kind of research from the perspective of purely explanatory standards. Himmilstein and Kimmel (1981) isolate what is probably Skocpol's greatest shortcoming: the failure to account for the processes which intervene between preconditions and outcomes. A structural perspective downgrades or excludes ideology, political organization, revolutionary elite activity (in the sense of day-to-day tactical and strategic choices), and other factors which surface in a 'voluntarist' or non-deterministic explanation. *Structural preconditions and human actions to convert the preconditions into outcomes are both indispensable ingredients of a valid theory of revolution.* Relatedly, the volitional element becomes even more significant when we consider less extreme forms of collective action and political instability.

We can catalog the limits and weaknesses of the 'structural' school as follows:

— a general neglect of dynamic processes—the 'black box' between 'inputs' (preconditions) and 'outputs' (revolutionary transformations and their consequences);
— a complete neglect of collective violence below the level of revolution (the very large iceberg below the very fundamental but very rare 'social revolution');
— a limited range of cases;
— ambiguity about the nature of the impact of agrarian structural factors on peasant revolutionary involvement;
— lack of consensus about the roles of political and military organizations (for example, are they autonomous causes or inevitable by-products?);
— the relevance of the theories to the current context; and
— the conditions for revolution in societies that are neither imperial–feudal (Eisenstadt) nor agrarian–absolutist–monarchical (Skocpol).

We should also note that there are many case studies of political instability which fall outside the boundaries of the

Moore–Wolf–Skocpol tradition. The literature on particular countries, areas, and revolutions (and other forms of instability) has accounted for the annihilation of more than a few forests. We have said nothing at all, for example, about the large published literature on fascism and its relation to political instability. (Merkl (1981) does an excellent job of guiding the reader through the current and recent literature on fascism, development, and instability, including the links between studies of fascism and several of the general books on instability.) Historical case studies of famous revolutions and other manifestations of instability are so numerous that we could not even begin to catalog them. The prolific output on modern guerrilla warfare ('limited war,' 'internal war,' or any one of a number of other generally equivalent labels) is another example. Orlansky (1970) presents a good review of this literature, which comes from the right, left, and center and appears in exhortatory/repressionist ('how I did it' and 'how I stopped it' manuals) as well as less ideological versions. Allan and Stahel (1983) cite the landmark guerrilla warfare studies.

We would like to briefly mention two very useful kinds of case studies on instability: 'theoretical' case studies and comparative case studies. A *theoretical case study* looks at one case (an incident, a country, a revolutionary leader or movement, or some other bounded subject) in an intensive (in-depth and at-length) fashion and examines one or more theoretical questions explicitly and systematically. George (1979) and many others demonstrate convincingly that case studies can be explanatory in the best sense of that term. *Comparative case studies* juxtapose two or more cases, using the basic logic fleshed out in Skocpol and Somers (1980) of trying to generalize without losing sight of the details and particulars of reality.

Markides and Cohn (1982) provide us with a good illustration of a theoretical case study. Quantitative researchers since the early 1960s have devoted a great deal of time and effort to studying the link between conflict within and between nations, but the results have been modest, disappointing, and confusing.[3] Markides and Cohn, in contrast, focus on a particular kind of external–internal conflict relationshp: external conflict as a determinant of internal cohesion. Using historical data from a case study on the political evolution of the Greek Cypriot community after the Turkish invasion of 1974, they re-evaluate the old idea that conflict from outside the group brings about unity within. They conclude that the relationship can be expected to hold when:

— political elites are unified enough to reach a consensus on how to deal with the conflict;
— there is a minimal consensus among the group members that a policy exists which can resolve the conflict; and
— in societies with deep political divisions, one side should not be able to blame the other for the emergence of the threat.

None of these three conditions held for the Greek Cypriot case.

Research on social movements, ethnicity, and terrorism could be used to illustrate comparative case studies. All three of these concepts are related to political instability, with instability often appearing as the result of the mobilization of a social movement, ethnicity frequently functioning as a source of instability, and terrorism representing a particular form of instability.[4] For example, Maatsch et al. (1980) inventory the available studies of social movements. They categorize the research into sources, processes, characteristics, and consequences of movements, and attempt to synthesize the existing literature into theories and typologies (categories) of movements. Drawing exclusively on published research, they summarize six diverse case studies:

— the Free Yemeni Movement;
— the Eritrean Liberation Front (ELF);
— ETA and the Basques;
— the Saya San Rebellion in Burma;
— the 1961 Rebellion in Angola; and
— the American Indian Ghost Dance Movement.

The Free Yemeni Movement concerns the process of mobilizing participants to join a Third World Islamic social movement. The movement (Ahrar), which lasted from 1940 to 1948 and is discussed in detail in al-Abdin (1979), assassinated the Imam of North Yemen, Yahya Hamid al-Din, in early 1948. Ahrar was at first accepted when it assumed power, but it failed to secure the support of the army and the warrior tribes. Crown Prince Ahmad mobilized these elements and crushed the revolt in March of 1948, one month after the assassination.

The Eritrean Liberation Front (ELF) is a classic Third World nationalistic-separatist movement. The ELF launched its first revolt against the central government of Ethiopia in 1961. Bell (1974) chronicles the trends for this 'endemic insurgency,' which flared and subsided several times during the early 1970s (and has reappeared since), attracting aid along the way from the Saudis, Syria, Nasser in Egypt, Nkrumah in Ghana, Sudan, and Libya.

While the ELF case shows how a separatist movement can become enmeshed in international politics, another separatist movement, ETA (Euzkadi to Azkatasuma) in the Basque region of Spain, provides an almost picture-perfect account of how a movement can be an outgrowth of a very long historical process and then degenerate into terrorism. Payne (1971) is the major source for the ETA case.

Adas (1979) reports on the Saya San Rebellion in Burma in his interesting study of revitalization movements, a millennarian-type force which appears in colonial agrarian societies under-going modernization. Rapid change, relative deprivation,[5] a charismatic leader, and a colonial bureaucracy can interact to bring about revolts such as the Saya San Rebellion, which went on from 1930 to 1932. Organized insurrections, outbursts of communal violence, and actions by bandit gangs marked the rebellion.

Paige (1975) is the source for the Angola case study; this was a one-month rebellion in March of 1961 in which the Portuguese colonial system and the introduction of a plantation system for growing and exporting coffee interacted with the traditional and nationalistic values of the northern Bakongo tribe. The tribe was the base of a rural, communal party that produced a high level of political mobilization in the area. The agrarian revolt was the result of wage laborers organized around a com-munal village structure opposed to the non-cultivator class, which derived its income from land—thereby meeting Paige's (1975) criteria for a revolutionary situation. After one month, the Portuguese crushed the revolt—though not permanently.

The American Indian Ghost Dance Movement study by Carroll (1975) relies on the concept of relative deprivation and the level of kinship ties within tribal Indian groups to explain the acceptance or rejection of a revitalization movement among Indians in the American West. Relative deprivation is relevant because the destruction of buffalo herds had created material hardship for tribes dependent on the buffalo for food and clothing. Since the destruction of the herds occurred over a period of twenty years, the length of time a tribe had to adjust to this deprivation affected the amount of deprivation which was felt. Northern tribes had less time to adjust and were therefore more likely to accept the doctrine of the Ghost Dance.

These cases demonstrate that social movements can arise from a variety of sources (nationalism, separatism, relative deprivation, economic relations and changes). In addition, the path which a movement takes once the mobilization process starts is determined by a variety of factors (ranging from charismatic leadership to the nature of the interaction between the movement and the regime). The case studies can be related to some of the major theoretical perspectives in the study of political instability, as illustrated in Table 2.1.

Table 2.1 arrays the six case studies against fifteen major theorists of instability, identifying areas of intersection where the case 'data' implicitly or explicitly draw on a particular perspective.

Ethnicity is an inescapable facet of politics within as well as between countries; internal conflict and instability and external

Table 2.1 Social Movements Case Studies and Instability Theorists

	ETA	ELF	Angola	Burma	North Yemen	Ghost Dance
de Tocqueville					X	
Davies			X			
Feierabends					X	
Huntington			X	X		
Dollard	X		X	X	X	X
Gurr			X	X		X
Smelser	X	X	X	X	X	X
Hagopian			X	X	X	
Johnson			X	X	X	
Oberschall				X	X	X
Tilly	X	X		X	X	X
McCarthy and Zald	X	X		X	X	X
Paige			X			
Adas				X		
Skocpol			X	X		

conflict and war often flow from ethnic tensions and processes of mobilization. Traditional Western development theory and Marxism converge in predicting that ethnicity will recede in importance as the modernization process accelerates. The resurgence of 'ethnopolitics' throughout the world in recent years contradicts what used to be the conventional wisdom in a direct and very compelling fashion. Boulding (1979) contends that ethnicity accounts for an increasing share of non-revolutionary violence and non-violent social movements. The Basques in Spain are only one of the many examples of ethnicity reasserting itself in the developed Western world. Other examples include the Flemings and Walloons in Belgium, the Bretons in France, the British Celtic fringe in Scotland, Northern Ireland, and Wales, and the French in Quebec.

Ethnic divisions are in fact a pervasive feature of all kinds of societies. Most nations in fact contain two or more 'nations.' Only thirteen countries fulfill the standards of ethnic homogeneity according to which over 95 percent of a group's membership lives in one country and the group also makes up 95 percent or more of that country's population (Nielsson, 1980). Aside from Taiwan, Hong Kong, and eleven other similarly homogeneous countries, all other nations show at least some ethnic diversity—and many have quite a bit. But do static differences frequently translate into politically active differences? Boulding (1979) discovers that ethnic communities and national and international separatist movements are concentrated in forty-four countries and consist of:

— seventy guerrilla movements or terrorist organizations in thirty-three countries, aimed at separatism or revolution;
— forty-seven national movements for separatism or cultural autonomy in fifteen countries; and
— sixty-five international organizations in twenty-one nations, supporting separatist movements or cultural autonomy.

Overall, there are over 6,800 ethnic communities in the world, with over 175 organizations actively representing the interests of the various ethnic groups.

The qualitative and quantitative research on ethnicity, ethnic mobilization, ethnic separatism and violence, and instability in general is voluminous. A lot of the quantitative work on ethnic mobilization uses data for political units within a country (for example, comparing voting returns for core and periphery counties in England). The results of the various statistical model tests are conflicting and confusing (Leifer 1981; Ragin 1979; Hechter 1975), although Nielsen (1980) represents something of an improvement. The quantitative research is especially weak for identifying and fleshing out the processes involved in ethnic mobilization.

This is where explanatory case studies—investigations of actual examples in detail and preferably across time—come into the picture. Jacob's (1981) case study of the Germanic minority in the South Tyrol of Italy chronicles the history of ethnic mobilization in this area and identifies the linguistic, geographic, and occupational sources of support for the pro-Germanic Sudtiroler Volkspartei (SVP). Jacob (1981) concludes by using the case study to identify a set of factors which are especially relevant to the comparative study of ethnic mobilization:

— The persistence of ethnic and linguistic loyalties.
— The interaction of religion and ethnicity, with religious identification acting as a powerful spur for ethnicity.
— The role of Austria, with its historic claims to the South Tyrol suggesting the importance of the presence on the border of an irredentist state.
— The crucial role of the state and public policy in the management of ethnic conflict, with the moderation of the SVP's ideology as a direct response to concessions made by the Italian state to satisfy both Austrians and South Tyroleans.

Some countries are so deeply divided by the presence of different ethnic communities that their very existence—their ultimate political stability—is called into question. Horowitz (1982) uses the concept of a 'dual authority polities' or countries deeply divided into two or more such communities to develop a framework for studying divided societies. He applies the overall approach to the four countries where the center (the government) and peripheries (the community levels) both had significant authority and he found that the common political system eventually collapsed:

— Palestine during the British Mandate;
— Cyprus;

— Lebanon; and
— Northern Ireland.

Interestingly, two of the cases—Palestine and Cyprus—involve divisions that are fundamentally ethnic, while Ireland and Lebanon feature a primarily religious division (with some ethnic connotations as well). Horowitz (1982) pinpoints various demographic, economic, political, and/or paramilitary shifts in the internal balance of power as the indicator which really signals the beginning of critical instability, the prelude to the disintegration of a society. The survival of the center relates to the preservation of the balance of authority between it and the respective communal centers. Such a balance is very much tied up with the political status quo. According to Horowitz (1982: 344), 'attempts to change the status quo are therefore apt to result not in a new balance-of-power formula, but rather in a more conflict-ridden political climate or even in the collapse of the system.'

Just as Skocpol (1979) juxtaposes positive and negative cases in the study of revolutions, Horowitz (1982) uses his overall conclusion about the intrinsic weakness of divided polities to discuss the need to identify the conditions which promote the survival of such countries. He urges the comparison of such nations with fairly stable 'divided' democratic systems, like Belgium. According to Horowitz, divided societies where communal affiliation is not related to territory can be compared with federal states that are bicommunal (Czechoslovakia, Canada) or multicommunal (Switzerland, Yugoslavia), and divided societies in Europe and the Middle East can be compared with divided societies in Asia (Malaysia, Pakistan before the creation of Bangladesh) and in Africa (Nigeria, Zimbabwe, South Africa).

Social movements and ethnicity are central concepts in the social sciences and both have spawned a large literature comprised of innumerable case studies, while the output in the study of *terrorism* is nothing short of explosive. Terrorism is dramatic, anxiety-provoking, and fascinating; terrorism researchers are also well-funded. Terrorism is a mass production industry desperately in need of more highly skilled analysts and researchers. Hopple (1982b) surveys the literature and relates it to political instability research. Reid (1983) offers a detailed bibliometric and content analytic study of terrorism.

The largest portion of the terrorist literature features case studies of particular countries, regions, movements, and even individual terrorists. The research is almost completely atheoretical, although so much substantive information is available that it should be possible to dissect it in a systematic and explicit way, compare cases, and develop some generalizations. Such significant theoretical questions include the transition from domestic to transnational terrorism and the effect of government repression on terrorism. The case study data would complement and enhance the extensive statistical data on terrorist events available in such compilations as the CIA's ITERATE (International Terrorism: Attributes of Terrorist Events) and similar data banks (CIA 1980; Mickolus 1978), and other government-funded data bases.

By way of summarizing this section, note that explanation is concerned with why and how political instability occurs. A great many qualitative analysts have grounded their ideas in historical notions about change and sociological approaches and methods. Many case studies have been produced within these guidelines.

Interestingly, the Marxist theory of revolution is a good example of a qualitative explanatory analysis. Relatedly, other analysts have based explanations upon the nature and activity of the agrarian, peasant, and/or disenfranchised social classes, just as many others attribute political instability and revolution to the behavior of the elites in society.

Others have approached the explanatory problem by analyzing whole civilizations across time and in parallel, while some base their ideas upon national structures, the impact of international events and conditions, and assumptions about the autonomy of the state.

Social movement research can be classified into research into the sources, processes, characteristics, and consequences of various movements.

Ethnicity can also be found at the center of many revolutionary episodes, and given the pervasiveness of ethnicity in the world, can be expected to continue to exert a profound impact upon social and political behavior.

Finally, qualitative explanations traceable to terrorist activity have proliferated at about the same rate that terrorist activity has increased. These explanations frequently combine elements from all of the qualitative approaches and methods that have been used to explain political violence.

Qualitative prediction

The qualitative predictive research in political instability presented below focuses upon the following areas, methods, and approaches:

— intuition and judgment;
— Delphi forecasting;
— cross-impact forecasting;
— Bayesian forecasting; and
— political risk assessment.

Humans are constantly trying to foresee and plan for the future. An entire forecasting industry has emerged in recent decades in response to this universal desire. The tools and techniques are many and varied and range from the qualitative to the quantitative. All qualitative forecasting rests ultimately on human judgments. Qualitative or expert-generated data may be intuitive in nature or may be based on any one of several more systematic techniques (Andriole 1983; Hopple and Kuhlman 1981).

Intuitive qualitative forecasting is central to intelligence analysis, and this is as true for assessing political instability as it is for other areas of intelligence. An individual immersed in the history, culture, and politics of a country or area generates estimates and projections on a continuing basis. There is no real substitute for such wisdom, insight, and intuition. There is, however, a stockpile of systematic analytical techniques that are useful for processing, refining, and restructuring human judgments. Such techniques, if used properly, can be very useful to the individual country or area analyst. They can confirm and crystallize, revise and refine, and serve as sounding boards or devil's advocates.*

This section briefly surveys some of the systematic qualitative approaches and documents a few examples of qualitative instability forecasting. *At the outset, we should emphasize that there are no absolutely reliable, fully validated, or foolproof analytical systems that can substitute for expertise.*

There are many potential partial aids and some untested or only partly tested models and methods.

There has been a great deal of political instability forecasting undertaken for private corporations concerned with foreign investment planning and decision-making. In recent years, a political risk 'industry' has mushroomed. Researchers from academia and government consultants have treated the private sector as a potential new arena for conducting interesting research. Many large multinational firms have their own in-house risk assessment staffs and centers, and several commercial potential risk services are available.

Political risk assessment and government instability analysis converge in a number of ways. Risk and intelligence analysts both monitor a complex environment and try to anticipate unfolding trends and warn of impending dangers or crises. Their shared real world orientation leads to a preoccupation with questions of utility, and their assessments and projections are inevitably concerned with achieving hits and avoiding false alarms. The two also generate reports which become part of a larger strategic or policy planning process.

Political risk analysis for the corporate sector has a long history. Traditionally, the approach has tasked experts (often overseas managers of the firm) to conduct 'case studies,' using a very intuitive or seat-of-the-pants strategy for scanning the political environment and generating forecasts (Haendel 1981). This is not at all unlike the process of traditional instability analysis. But more recently there has been some interest in more systematic methods. Often, this simply means the explicit consideration of rudimentary political risk checklists which specify different types of instability and list a set of relevant environmental factors; few multinationals use formal, well-developed techniques (Kobrin *et al.* 1980).

There has been very little work with quantitative political risk systems. By 'quantitative' in this context we mean objective and statistical. Haendel (1979) describes an indicator-based system consisting of three types of data: socio-economic characteristics, social conflict, and governmental processes. Socio-economic indicators include GNP growth rates and ethnic diversity. Societal conflict is comprised of such acts of internal conflict as riots, demonstrations, and armed attacks. Governmental processes refer to political competition, yearly political changes, and legislative effectiveness. The various indicators are put together to yield Political System Stability Index (PSSI) scores for Third World countries, with nations ranked from low to high. (We will discuss a whole host of quantitative indicators later in the book.) Another example of the use of objective data is *Euromoney's* country risk rating based on loan spreads.

Experts are the data sources in most risk systems. This is true of Haner's (1975) Business Environment Risk Index (BERI) and other risk assessment services which elicit opinions from panels of experts. Many of these rely on the Delphi method for forecasting. Delphi, which was developed at the Rand Corporation in the early 1950s, has been used in several thousand diverse forecasting applications throughout the world (Helmer 1978). The *Delphi method* is a way of making 'soft' or expert data reliable. The procedure blends anonymity (to prevent bias and minimize the impact of powerful panel members) with the dynamism of a debate. A panel of experts is polled in a series of questionnaires. At the end of each session, feedback is given to the panelists regarding the response distributions and the arguments offered in favor of deviant positions. Average group judgments from the final round usually serve as the final data.

Haner's BERI Index is based on a Delphi procedure for assessing the general political climate in many countries. Indices representing both short- and long-term political risk are constructed. Coplin and O'Leary's World Political Risk Forecasts (WPRF), marketed by Frost and Sullivan, Inc., are basically similar to BERI. Both a world summary, updated on a monthly basis, and detailed country reports are available to clients for a fee.

One of the more sophisticated expert-based approaches is the Shell Oil System (Gebelein *et al.* 1978). The Shell or ASPRO method (Assessment of Probabilities) provides a technique for systematically reviewing all factors considered important to an uncertain event. ASPRO elicits opinions via a questionnaire. Experts are asked to consider each factor that affects a proposition and to judge the extent to which the factor holds or does not hold. The expert also gives his degree of confidence in the judgment. Propositions relate to the occurrence of an undesirable event. An example is the likelihood of adverse tax rates on a country over the next ten years.

This is another subjective forecasting method useful for political instability analysis. The cross-impact method provides a way of determining with probability how a change in one event or condition will affect other events and conditions (Andriole 1983). It allows for a systematic assessment of how 'everything affects everything else.' The steps required to implement the method include the following:

- list all relevant events or conditions;
- estimate the probability of each one;
- construct what is called a probability cross-impact matrix (see Figure 2.6);
- for each pair of events, estimate the conditional probability (the probability of the first event if the second one occurs); and
- calculate (usually on a computer) the event likelihoods given the initial event and paired event probabilities.

Moritz (1978) reports a CIA example of cross-impact analysis, using forecasts for Rhodesia generated during a week in April 1976. The participants first produced a list of events whose

If This Event Occurs	Initial Prob- ability	The Probability of This Event Becomes:							
		1	2	3	4	5	6	7	8
EVENT 1		■							
EVENT 2			■						
EVENT 3				■					
EVENT 4					■				
EVENT 5						■			
EVENT 6							■		
EVENT 7								■	
EVENT 8									■

Fig. 2.6 Cross-Impact Matrix

occurrence would exert an impact on the overall Rhodesian situation. The analysts assigned initial probabilities to each event and then decided how the occurrence of each event would change the initial probability for every other event (see Figure 2.6). The computer output reported the final event probabilities. For example, for the event 'significant increase in Communist assistance to the insurgents,' the initial probability of 0.40 increased to 0.70 as the result of the effect of nine other events (including direct South African and communist troop intervention and an increase in fighting because of economic costs).

In addition to Delphi and cross-impact forecasting, quite a few examples of *Bayesian forecasting* are available (Andriole 1981, 1983; Heuer 1978; Hopple and Kuhlman 1981). Bayesian analysis has served as the foundation for a number of computer-based decision analysis and forecasting aids. These have been applied to a number of actual cases of international conflict and crisis and internal instability forecasting. Bayesian inference involves a mathematical procedure for revising probability judgments on the basis of new information. Experts are asked to make conditional probability judgments for each relevant item of evidence. The expert is asked: given the truth of the hypothesis, what is the probability of seeing the evidence? The heart of Bayesian analysis is a formula developed by the Reverend Bayes in the 1730s to take an initial probability and change it into a revised one. There are at least three variations on the Bayesian analytical theme. The first involves the application of Bayes' theorem of conditional probabilities for updating estimates in the light of new information, as suggested briefly above. The second involves structuring the forecasting problem into an 'influence diagram' which portrays the forecasting objective as 'driven' or 'influenced' by individual or interrelated sets of variables; while the third is much more complicated, assuming aspects of the first and second themes. Known as cascaded or hierarchical inference structuring, this technique enables a forecaster to decompose hierarchically and systematically aspects of the forecasting object that are interrelated and interdependent. Figure 2.7 presents a graphical Bayesian update of the events that led to the Soviet invasion of Czechoslovakia in 1968. Figure 2.8 illustrates how an influence diagram can be constructed, while Figure 2.9 illustrates how a hierarchical inference structure can be developed

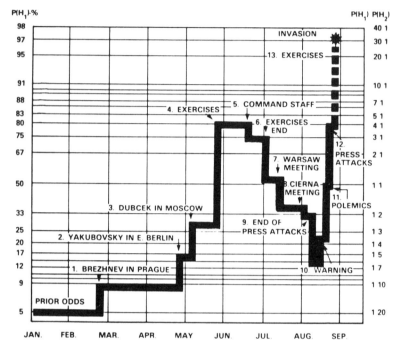

Fig. 2.7 Bayesian Update of Czechoslovakian Invasion (showing percentage likelihood on left and odds on right)

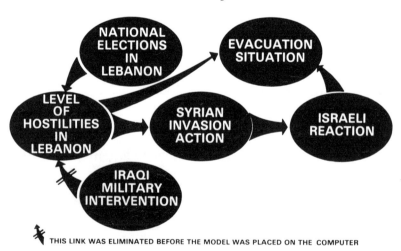

THIS LINK WAS ELIMINATED BEFORE THE MODEL WAS PLACED ON THE COMPUTER

Fig. 2.8 Evacuation Situation Influence Diagram

HYPOTHESES

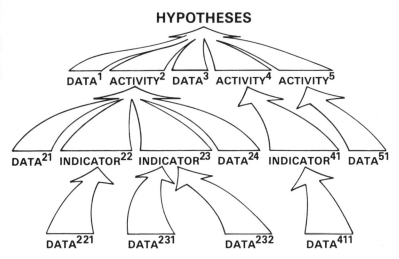

Fig.2.9 Hierarchical Inference Structure

(Barclay *et al.* 1977). Note how the hypotheses at the top of the structure are inferentially affected by the interrelationships among data, activities, and indicators.

In a project for the US Department of Defense, Duncan and Job (1980) use Bayesian analysis for short-term forecasting with expert judgments. They combine a statistical forecasting methodology with Bayesian procedures to produce a series of forecasts about the expected changes in the relationship between two conflicting parties. Specifically, they assess the probability of moving from one status to another in an immediate future (for example, from no tension to minor tension, from open hostility to war). One of their case studies is Israel and Syria, a classic international politics conflict situation. Another is Rhodesia, an equally dramatic example of extreme political instability within a nation—civil war. The basic outline of the Duncan-Job strategy includes the following steps:

— Select the situation of concern to the forecast and identify the relevant conditions—the 'states' of the situation (for example, transitions from low level violence to civil war or from civil war to peace).
— Elicit the analyst's initial assessments of the likelihood of changes in the status of their situation.
— Monitor the situation on a daily basis.

- Update and revise the analyst's assessments as necessary.
- Produce short-term, real-time probability forecasts (for example, over the next thirty days).
- If necessitated by changes in the environment, change the analyst's subjective judgments.

Although the statistical details of the approach are quite complex, the Duncan–Job forecasting system is completely computer-based. It has been used to forecast short-term change in Poland (in a special project for the Defense Intelligence Agency) as well as Rhodesia in the early 1980s. The approach blends expert judgments with Bayesian and other statistical routines in a fashion that makes the analyst's forecasting systematic, but it does not fundamentally change the normal manner in which the analyst functions. One drawback, however, is that the analyst must understand and be able to work with the fairly advanced statistical concepts involved.

Qualitative forecasting relies directly on expertise and thus keeps the analyst centrally involved. This is good for two reasons. First, 'objective' data are often suspect and are rarely available on a frequent, real-time basis. The quantitative indicator systems discussed in detail later are often several—or more—years behind. *Secondly, analysts are often skeptical about (or openly hostile toward) quantitative forecasting with objective data and techniques like regression analysis and causal modeling.* There is certainly no guarantee that analysts or consumers will embrace systematic expert-based forecasts with any enthusiasm or even tolerance. But the prospects are at least not quite as bleak.

We conclude with several very important warnings. First, the lack of validation of expert-based forecasts is shocking. Everyone forecasts, but very few go back and check the forecasts. There have been efforts in this direction, but they are few and far between. The political risk systems are no better in this respect. Since the commercial services are proprietary and the in-house operations private, no one keeps score. We also have some reservations about the use of qualitative or expert data for political instability forecasting, because a lot of evidence indicates that people are prone to all kinds of biases and systematic errors when they process information and make judgments. Experts may not be immune to these problems.[6] When we compare experts who make judgments about political affairs within or between countries, we find that they disagree much more than they agree. There has been very little research on this, but the little that has been conducted shows that experts disagree quite a bit—even when the experts are all very well qualified academic or intelligence area and country specialists making judgments about very important conditions and events.[7] People simply disagree about what reality is.

Furthermore, there is enormous support for the superior performance of statistical models over humans when it comes to forecasting certain kinds of phenomena. Experts may know which factors are important, but they are consistently out-performed by statistical models when they are required to put it all together and generate actual forecasts. This holds for trained clinicians classifying patients, university admissions committee members predicting student grade point averages, and in many other areas. *Whether the disparity is as consistent or as large in political instability forecasting is an open question at this point.*

These caveats are not offered to set up a straw man to belittle intuition—there is hardly any evidence that quantitative forecasts do better (or as well). But we do strongly recommend that the political instability analyst zealously follow a *caveat emptor* strategy when evaluating instability forecasts.

In summary, we should not lose sight of the fact that those who have attempted to predict political instability have used a variety of methods, approaches, and techniques all more or less grounded in the generation and assessment of expert data. Experts use their experience, intuition, and judgment to make often impressively accurate forecasts. At the same time, it is often very difficult to understand how or why such forecasts are accurate.

Political risk assessment is but one area to which judgmental forecasting methods have been applied. Usually country experts are used to generate country forecasts; sometimes the experts reside in the target country while sometimes they generate forecasts remotely via secondary sources.

Delphi, cross-impact, and Bayesian forecasting methods are sometimes used to systematically produce and validate forecasts. The Delphi method involves assembling and polling experts in a series of forecasting 'rounds.' Cross-impact methods require the forecaster to make forecasts given the occurrence likelihood of other interrelated events. Bayesian methods are rooted in Bayes' theorem of conditional probabilities, a theorem which enables forecasters to revise initial probabilities in the light of new information. Bayes' theorem can be used all by itself, in conjunction with influence diagrams, or as the pivot around which hierarchical inference structures can be implemented.

All qualitative forecasting methods and techniques are only as good as the subjective estimates of the expert forecasters. Some are very good, but some hold biased views which may or may not be known to the expert. Finally, research in comparative forecasting suggests that experts frequently generate extremely different forecasts even when using identical methods.

3 Quantitative political instability analysis

Quantitative approaches to the study of political instability apply one or more statistical techniques to the analytical goals of describing, explaining, or predicting instability. Andriole (1983) inventories and describes the major quantitative analytical methodologies. Useful reviews of quantitative instability research include Goldstone (1980), Gurr (1980), Muller (1977), Sanders (1981), Snyder (1978), and Tilly (1975, 1978).

Quantitative description

Quantitative descriptive research has generally focused upon the following:

— The development of definitions of political instability grounded in empirical 'counts' of various conflictual events and conditions.
— The development of empirical distinctions among 'political instability,' 'political crises,' 'collective political violence,' 'rebellion,' and 'protest.'
— Event data-based definitions of political instability.
— The development of quantitative indicators of political instability.
— The development of computer-based 'early warning' and monitoring systems, grounded in domestic event data, designed to track political instability and domestic violence.
— The development of 'Internal Situation Profiles' (ISPs) of potential domestic stress.
— The development of governmental change indices.
— Quantitative descriptions of terrorist-based and induced instability.
— The assembly of computer-based quantitative data bases on terrorist and counter-terrorist activity.

Any phenomenon can be described via definition, decomposition, and classification. There have been many efforts to define political instability, generate typologies, and profile instability in terms of its frequency, intensity, and the like. Definitions of political instability have been identified with the study of civil strife, mass political violence (versus coups and other kinds of elite instability), intrasocietal conflict, internal war, civil war, and guerrilla warfare. Morrison and Stevenson (1971: 348) exemplify a common tendency to define political instability as a situation in which institutionalized authority patterns in a nation break down and political violence replaces compliance with political authorities. This definition leads to a concern with the more extreme or threatening forms of instability. When instability reaches this point, it represents a *crisis* for a nation and its rulers.

Crisis has been a central analytical focus—especially in the study of international politics (Hopple and Rossa 1981; Hopple *et al*. 1983). The crisis concept has a lot of siblings, including stress, conflict, tension, panic, catastrophe, and disaster (Robinson 1972: 25). Stress is particularly associated with the crisis concept. Milburn (1972: 262), for example, views a crisis as a 'stress-producing stimulus.' A political instability crisis places a great deal of stress on a country's political system. In international politics, crisis is a turning point, a critical juncture which straddles the boundary between war and peace. Analogously, a political instability crisis appears when a critical point is reached—where the clear and inescapable choice is between routine CA (ordinary processes of conflict and cooperation, with or without violence) and the alternatives of basic system change or successful conflict resolution (or repression of the opposition).

A political instability crisis relates directly to political performance, a nation's legitimacy, and its persistence. Governmental repression, performance, legitimacy, persistence, political violence, and political instability crises are core concepts for monitoring, explaining, and forecasting political instability (Zimmermann 1979a: 76). (We will return to the coercion-performance-legitimacy issue later.)

Conceptually, then, political instability equals collective political violence. All collective action is either cooperative or conflictual. Conflict—the situation where two or more individuals or groups are seeking incompatible or mutually exclusive goals—is normal and pervasive in domestic politics. Political violence is a subset of political conflict, and the political instability crisis is a subset of political violence. Figure 3.1, which builds on an earlier figure, represents our conceptual treatment of political instability (the portion of the figure which is boxed off).

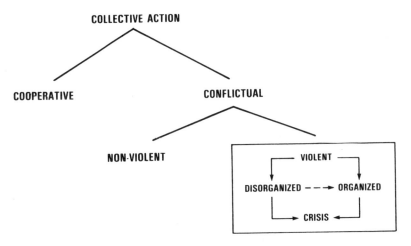

Fig.3.1 Organized/Disorganized Violence Model of Instability

It is generally agreed that political instability has more than one facet. Rummel (1963) was the first of many quantitative-explanatory theorists to build upon the pioneering work of Raymond Cattell (who searched for general cultural patterns across societies) and try to identify some basic dimensions of domestic and foreign conflict. Rummell and his many successors have used factor analysis, a statistical technique which is designed to reduce many relationships to a few central patterns. The many specific studies are summarized in Orlansky (1970), Morrison and Stevenson (1971), Sanders (1981), and Stohl (1980). Generally, domestic conflict breaks down into two broad types, internal war or rebellion (the organized dimension in Figure 3.1) and collective protest (the disorganized/spontaneous dimension). These are the two general dimensions which are analyzed in the models of Hibbs (1973) and Gurr and Duvall (1973).

In terms of individual participation, one can draw a broad distinction between democratic and aggressive participation (Muller 1977, 1979, 1980). Democratic participation encompasses cooperative (and non-violent conflictual) collective action; aggressive participation includes both non-violent (for example, civil disobedience) and violent collective action. (Research on individual aggressive participation will be summarized later in the book.)

This discussion has submerged some very necessary but arcane measurement issues (Jacobson 1973b). We will not go into detail here, but it should be noted that all kinds of measurement, sampling, and other problems pervade the quantitative analysis of political instability. We raise the issue here not only because of its intrinsic importance but to illuminate two further points. First, it is amazing how often these kinds of concerns are neglected. Linehan (1976) maintains that the many factor analysis studies may be 'wrong' because they used raw event frequencies (the actual counts of what happened) rather than per capita frequencies, which take population into account (and thereby prevent six riots in Chad and China from being counted as 'equal'). Secondly, statistical issues are rarely straightforward. Statisticians argue as much as any analytical group. For example, Linehan (1976) applies a very sophisticated technique to some instability data and finds only one general dimension. But his results are suspect for two reasons. First, we have some real reservations about using such a powerful technique with such soft data. Secondly, there are theoretical reasons for supporting the idea of dividing instability into two types, especially if the overall view is one like ours which defines instability as violent collective action. If, in other words, you look only at instability, it may all look similar (and may fall on the same dimension). If you look at instability in the context of all political conflict and collective behavior in general, then it becomes important to make any distinctions that do exist. The fact that a considerable amount of research shows that 'causes' associated with protest are much different from those which 'explain' rebellion suggests that the two are not the same.

As suggested earlier, a great deal of instability research has taken an *event approach*. An event is a specific action defined on the basis of an actor, a target, and a form of behaviour. This who-does-what-to-whom format is used to organize activity into many discrete and specific actions. Event data may be taken from any kind of a source which reports 'news.' The methodology is the same whether the source is public (for example, a newspaper or news chronology), private, or classified. Events are collected by using systematic and replicable rules for converting the verbal material that normally appears in the source into coded data that can be retrieved from a computer. The actual process is straightforward but laborious.

In international politics, some event data sets attempt to reflect all visible activity of a non-routine nature between governments and other international actors. The activity is usually measured in terms of total volume and such breakdowns as cooperation and conflict. Many event data bases are available. One of the best-known is the World Event Interaction Survey (WEIS), which has been studied extensively for basic and applied research purposes and consists of over 100,000 events taken from the *New York Times* from the middle 1960s through 1981. The WEIS effort, initially sponsored by the Defense Department as a basic research endeavor, became the foundation for the Early Warning and Monitoring System, a computer-based information retrieval system which was developed and tested from 1976 to 1981. (The latter phase of the project moved beyond the *New York Times* to include other newspaper data as well as Foreign Broadcast Information Service and cable traffic data.) An example of using event data for the purpose of profiling or describing is presented in Figure 3.2, which shows total, cooperative, and conflictual behavior between Ethiopia and Somalia from the beginning of 1977 through the middle of 1978.

The many *domestic event data banks* used to study political instability consist mainly of counts of domestic conflict events (number of assassinations, number of general strikes, number of purges, and so forth); Gurr (1974a) discusses some of the major examples. Starting in the early 1970s, the Defense Advanced Research Projects Agency (DARPA), which sponsored WEIS as well as many of the other quantitative data collection efforts, launched a research program designed to evaluate the use of quantitative indicators for defense and national security analysis.

Spector *et al.* (1975) report on research which developed and

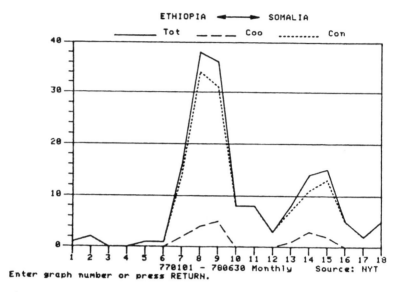

Fig. 3.2 Event Data Graph (Computer-Generated)

tested a set of international, economic, and internal indicators. The internal indicators measured:

— the domestic issue content of events;
— the behavior tone of bureaucratic and intragovernmental forces, as well as political parties and interest groups; and
— popular approval and disapproval of government positions and performance.

The event-based domestic indicators were evaluated as predictors of international behavior for Japan. Generally, domestic concern over resource dependency and domestic economic conditions showed the most influence on the quality of relations between Japan and other countries.

The research conducted by Spector provided the foundation for a series of domestic event data projects. In all of these cases, the basic approach was to identify major actors and targets within countries and monitor their interactions with each other. Trends across time within countries in terms of total activity, conflict activity, amount of tension, and numerous other event-based indicators were identified. Slater and Orloski (1978) summarized the results of the Governmental Indicators Change

Project on Peru and several other Latin American countries, conducted for the CIA by Mathtech, Inc. DARPA also sponsored research on politics within African countries which, like the Mathtech work, used a modified WEIS approach to study events within countries. This African Warning and Monitoring System was architecturally based on the international Early Warning and Monitoring System; both are described in Hopple (1980a). An example of output from the African system appears in Figure 3.3.

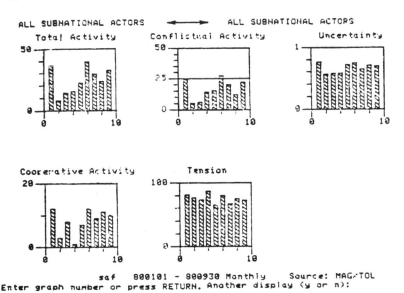

Fig. 3.3 Africa Early Warning and Monitoring System Output

The domestic event data approach has proved to be of some value for monitoring or describing political instability trends. Overall, however, the experience with domestic event data has been disappointing. We can offer the following net assessment:

— The approach has been adequate for descriptive purposes (information retrieval and monitoring), but weak for explanation and prediction.
— The event strategy 'forces' domestic politics into an actor-event-target 'straight jacket' which fits much less well for domestic than international politics.

— The approach reflects the entire range of behavior within a nation across the collective action continuum. In contrast, the basic research in the 1960s and early 1970s—the source of dozens of studies—focuses exclusively on domestic conflict and thereby made it impossible to develop a baseline or compare conflictual with cooperative activity.
— Domestic event data schemes are only as good as the sources on which they are based.

The source issue has been of particular concern and deserves a brief mention. Many source comparisons have appeared in both international politics and internal political instability research. Various elite newspapers (especially but not only the *New York Times*) and news almanacs and chronologies have been compared. Global and regional sources have also been evaluated comparatively. For studying international politics, it seems advisable to rely on two separate but generally good sources and compare them explicitly and systematically (Hopple 1982a). No source mirrors reality. All sources are selective and 'biased.' The really important question is whether the sources of quantitative data on internal conflict and violence are fundamentally and systematically biased. Zimmermann (1980) summarizes the research on sources. One study weighs the costs and benefits of multiple source usage and concludes that source differences do not apparently affect the overall nature of substantive results (Jackman and Boyd 1979). However, there has been very little research which determines the actual impact of source differences on findings about instability (as opposed to simpler research which compares reported frequencies of events and distributions by type and generally finds that sources do vary).

An example of a descriptive approach which is not based on domestic events is the *Internal Situation Profile or ISP* (Hopple 1978). What are the specific factors which tap the concept of 'potential domestic stress?' This question constituted the basis for a study to develop a set of internal indicators which would function together as an overall 'thermometer' for a political system. At the same time, the profiling scheme was designed to avoid the rigid event data approach, which narrowly limits indicators to those which can be derived from an actor–event–target scheme. A list of sixty-seven discrete indicators was developed (fifteen economic, twelve societal, seven military, twelve governmental, and twenty-one political). Some of the measures reflect domestic events or occurrences; others tap aspects or dimensions of situational contexts. The ISP is designed to monitor simultaneously three distinct sets of events and situations:

— preconditions for internal crises;
— precipitants (immediate determinants) of internal crises; and
— manifestations of internal crises.

ISP data were collected from the source *Facts on File* for seven countries (Peru, France, the Soviet Union, Zaïre, Egypt, India, and the Philippines) for the years 1966, 1970, and 1975. Item totals for each country and years are presented in Table 3.1.

Table 3.1 Item totals for ISP by state and year

STATE	1966		1970		1975		TOTALS	
Peru	2	(0.3%)	43	(5.4)	53	(6.6)	98	(12.2)
France	18	(2.2)	34	(4.2)	127	(15.9)	179	(22.4)
USSR	23	(2.9)	59	(7.4)	62	(7.7)*	144	(18.0)
Zaïre	28	(3.5)	19	(2.4)	16	(2.0)	63	(7.9)
Egypt	5	(0.6)	9	(1.1)	13	(1.6)	27	(3.4)
India	53	(6.6)	64	(8.0)	92	(11.5)	209	(26.1)
Philippines	1	(0.1)	58	(7.2)	21	(2.6)	80	(10.0)
Total	130	(16.2)	286	(35.7)	384	(47.9)	800	(100.0)

* 1976 for USSR.
Source: Facts on File.

In Table 3.2, the ISP items are rearranged into eleven general categories. These include two which refer to economic factors (international and domestic economic health), one which brings together a variety of domestic issue areas (social policy assessment), and a single item natural disasters category. There are also two government repression clusters (or group and individual rights), two mass activism domains (activities against the regime and mass protests), a government change category, a measure of government economic intervention, and an index which refers to ethnic and other divisive political tendencies. The many

Table 3.2 Weighted Internal Situation Profile index scores (by state and year)

	Philippines			USSR			Zaïre		
	1966	1970	1975	1966	1970	1975	1966	1970	1975
International economic health	0	1	0	1	2	3	0	1	-2
Domestic economic health	0	-2	0	0	0	-1	0	0	0
Social policy assessment	0	1	0	0	0	0	0	0	0
Natural disaster	0	6	3	1	1	3	1	0	0
Government repression of individual rights	0	5	0	3	7	1	3	1	1
Government repression of group rights	0	3	1	5	4	2	1	1	1
Anti-regime activities	0	6	1	0	0	0	-1	0	0
Mass protest	0	15	2	0	2	1	0	0	0
Governmental change	0	2	2	5	5	3	12	7	2
Governmental economic intervention	0	0	0	0	0	0	1	1	1
Centrifugal political tendencies	0	0	3	1	1	0	0	0	0

	Egypt (UAR)			France			India			Peru		
	1966	1970	1975	1966	1970	1975	1966	1970	1975	1960	1970	1975
International economic health	0	−1	0	1	1	4	0	1	0	0	1	0
Domestic economic health	0	0	−1	1	0	−15	0	1	−1	0	0	−1
Social policy assessment	0	0	0	2	0	2	−1	0	1	0	0	0
Natural disaster	0	0	0	0	7	2	1	2	2	2	4	0
Government repression of individual rights	0	0	2	−3	3	3	6	5	11	0	3	4
Government repression of group rights	0	0	1	0	0	1	5	2	14	0	2	6
Anti-regime activities	0	0	0	0	6	11	4	3	6	0	0	3
Mass protest	0	0	2	0	5	18	8	5	8	0	2	2
Governmental change	2	7	5	1	1	2	7	20	18	0	1	11
Governmental economic intervention	1	0	0	2	0	9	0	0	1	0	11	1
Centrifugal political tendencies	0	0	0	0	1	3	4	5	2	0	0	0

zeroes undoubtedly reflect the limitations of a single source. However, certain patterns can be seen. Among these are:

— The increase from 0 (1966) to 11 (1970) and then a decrease to 1 for government economic intervention in Peru.
— The increases from 6 to 11 (anti-regime acts) and 5 to 18 (mass protest) in France from 1970 to 1975.
— The precipitous drop in domestic economic health in France (from 1 to 0 to −15) across the three years.
— The upsurge in reported government repression items in India for both scales from the 1970 to 1975 points.
— The relatively and consistently high frequencies of anti-regime activities, mass protests, and divisive centrifugal political tendencies in India.
— The unusual frequency of mass protest in the Philippines in 1970.

Trends across time for a single country and comparative trends among nations can be plotted to depict changes in system performance and to estimate the amount of stress which some countries seem to experience continuously (such as India) or periodically (such as France).

Mention should also be made of the many cross-national data banks available for describing political instability. The updated third edition of the *World Handbook of Political and Social Indicators* has added new base dates (1970 and 1975) to the older ones (1950, 1955, 1960, and 1965) and the political events part of the data set now spans the period 1948 through 1977 (Taylor and Jodice 1980). Gurr (1974a) also describes and assesses the major data banks.

A lot of information is thus readily available for describing and statistically profiling political instability. We can easily look at patterns which show the distribution of various forms of political violence across time and by country and region. Gurr and Bishop (1976) furnish an example of such quantitative description. Their research is based on a typology of violence within and between nations. Violence may be overt and physical or covert (what they call 'patterns of denial' or the lack of minimal human needs, the denial of autonomy to groups within society, and so forth). Physical violence may be private or official in nature. Violence may occur within countries (as individual and collective violence) or between countries. Shown below is the overall Gurr–Bishop violence typology. On the basis of the typology, Gurr and Bishop (1976) generate data for all kinds of indicators of violence and then use factor analysis to reduce the many indicators to several central dimensions. They rank all 86 countries in their sample on the structure and physical violence scales.

— Physical/private/individual violence: suicide, homicide;
— physical/official/individual violence: arrests, executions;
— structural/coercive/individual violence: military/police size;
— structural/denied/individual violence: lack of basic services;
— physical/private/collective violence: protests, riots;
— structural/denied/collective violence: discrimination against subgroups;
— physical/private/transnational violence: terrorism;
— physical/official/transnational violence: war; and
— structural/denied/transnational violence: foreign exploitation.

Sanders (1981) develops a conceptual framework for measuring instability quantitatively which assumes that stability/instability is a continuous, interval level phenomenon. Using monthly *World Handbook* data from 1948–1967, he operationalizes four dimensions of instability: regime change, government change, violent challenge, and peaceful challenge. The data are standardized to capture the fact that instability is a short-term political situation of uncertainty (as opposed to cross-sectional models, where instability is treated as a long-term pattern) which displays different 'normalities' by system and time. Any particular event, in other words, should be regarded in the light of the extent to which it represents an abnormal deviation from a particular spatio-temporal pattern. Coups may be normal in Peru but highly irregular or unprecedented in Canada; a *coup d'état* in Canada would have a strikingly high z-score or deviation from normality, whereas coups in many Latin American and African nations are virtually routine. Similarly, violent challenges may be common in India but extremely rare in Denmark. The assumption that stability/instability is a continuum represents an improvement over the more popular premise that stable politics and instability are orthogonal and fits with many of the qualitative models described elsewhere in the book. The system-specific data transformations key the indicators to the particular context in which instability unfolds, yielding a framework around which the instability may be 'understood' and explained. In any case, it is important to recognize the differences between the two general schools of thought.

'Simple description' is an essential task. We cannot really explain or predict something unless we can describe it clearly and accurately. Like any phenomenon, political instability must be defined, classified into types, and profiled statistically. But even if we do not move beyond description, careful, accurate, and reliable descriptive characterization can be of inestimable value. Fairly recently, for example, the event data methodology has been adapted to the area of transnational terrorism, supplementing the traditional literature review and interview approaches (CIA 1980: 9). Quite a bit of descriptive data is now available on general trends in terrorism deaths and injuries across time, the geographical distribution of attacks, the nationality of victims, and so forth.

In a discussion of patterns of domestic terrorism in 87 countries in the late 1960s, Gurr (1979: 23) begins by cataloging some of the truisms about terrorism. For example, it is said that political terrorism is 'a relatively new strategy, one that has been resorted to especially by alienated, youthful members of the middle classes, and it has been increasing rapidly throughout the world.' 'It is an especially threatening form of political violence because of its destructiveness and potential revolutionary effects.' These and several other statements are all found to be false generalizations. Gurr (1979) proceeds to describe overall *patterns of domestic terrorism* in the 1960s and also profiles the characteristics of terrorist movements and of the objectives of terrorists.

In summary, please make special note that definitions of political instability have been developed by a whole host of analysts who have adopted just as many analytical perspectives. Some analysts define instability as a situation which involves the breakdown of national and societal institutional processes. A more serious form of instability is the intranational crisis, where a nation's political performance, legitimacy, and persistence are all threatened.

Measurement issues and problems surround all of the attempts to define quantitatively all aspects of political instability. It should always be remembered that statistics is as inexact a field of inquiry as virtually all of the social and behavioural sciences, liberal arts, and engineering sciences. There is nothing at all magical about the use of quantitative measures or their statistical manipulation. As a matter of fact, when used improperly statistics can confuse even the simplest of ideas.

The collection of event data for the study of political instability has grown out of the international event data movement and has concentrated on the collection of data that reflect the number of assassinations, strikes, purges, and the like that occur within a country. Relatedly, analysts have developed quantitative indicators of instability which in some cases represent aggregated event data types while in others do not. At least one of these event data/indicator 'systems' has been computerized in an experimental tool capable of storing, retrieving, and displaying intranational event data. But by and large such data and systems are much better suited to descriptive purposes than to any others; in fact, they are only adequate describers because event data 'straightjacket' intranational activity into categories that can be very unrepresentative of what is actually occurring within a country. Event data also tend to reflect the biases inherent in their source.

Yet another descriptive tool for analyzing political instability is the Internal Situation Profile, or ISP, which uses a set of descriptors to determine the 'health' of a nation at a particular point in time. From the ISP it is possible to develop governmental change indices which reflect aggregated changes in the ISPs of individual or groups of countries.

The data necessary to develop ISPs, governmental change indices, and similar descriptors of political instability are widely available, but not always reliable or continuous. Of particular contemporary interest are the data sets on terrorist events which have been used to profile terrorist groups, movements, and objectives.

Quantitative explanation

Explanatory studies of political instability which fall into the quantitative category tend to do one of two things: they either evaluate specific propositions or build and test elaborate 'causal models' of instability. The propositional studies often consider only one or a few determinants at a time, while the large models can become so complex that they defy clear interpretation.

This section looks at these two general classes of quantitative explanatory research. The specific foci include the following:

— research into the 'persistence' of political instability;
— economic sources of political instability, including short-term economic change, the overall level of economic development, the rate of economic growth, and socio-economic inequality;
— societal sources of instability, such as cleavages and modernization;
— political development sources, such as the level of democratization in a nation;
— sources traceable to a nation's political performance and perceived legitimacy;
— sources traceable to relative deprivation, frustration, and citizenry beliefs about violence;
— sources traceable to elite behavior, such as elite-based coups and repression;
— sources traceable to outside (international) variables, such as economic penetration, war, economic dependency; and
— causal models of instability.

(All of these 'sources' are also organized below in a way which permits their use as a blueprint for this lengthy section.)

Most of the research covered in this subsection is indebted to Durkheim, who attributed collective action to processes of integration and disintegration in whole societies (Tilly 1978). Durkheim distinguished between routine and non-routine contexts. The disintegration in society flows largely from the increased division of labor and a variety of undesirable results, including individual disorientation, destructive social life, and conflict. For Durkheim, the route to political instability is from the division of labor to discontent and then to deviant collective action. Aya (1979) refers to this as the volcanic model of collective violence. Figure 3.4 presents Durkheim's model.

We can distinguish between quantitative explanatory theories which rely on factors within countries to account for instability, and those which emphasize external or extranational determinants. The intranational–extranational distinction will be used

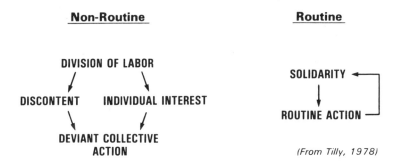

Fig. 3.4 Durkheim's Model of Collective Action/Instability

to organize this section. The general and specific categories appear as follows.

ORGANIZATION OF EXPLANATORY VARIABLES

I. Intranational
  A. Persistence Models
  B. Economic Factors
    1. Short-term economic change
    2. Level of economic development/modernization
    3. Growth rate
    4. Socio-economic inequality
  C. Societal
    1. Cleavages within society
    2. Structural imbalances
    3. Modernization
  D. Political Development
    1. Democratization
    2. Durability
  E. Performance and legitimacy
  F. Internal political processes
  G. Psychological-aggregate (mass politics)
    1. Deprivation/frustration
    2. Beliefs about violence
    3. Democratic and aggressive participation
  H. Elite Politics
    1. Elite instability/coups
    2. Repression
    3. Attitudes and belief systems
    4. Terrorism

II. Extranational
   A. Diffusion/contagion
   B. Economic and political penetration
      1. Foreign conflict
      2. War
      3. Dependency
III. General Models
   A. Hibbs
   B. Gurr and associates

The 'dependent variable'—that which we wish to explain—
is political instability. The factors listed above represent various
possible 'independent variables' or determinants of instability.
Some form of explanatory–statistical analysis has been used to
test hypotheses or models about each of the determinants in
relation to instability. The specific techniques have included:

— Correlation analysis (measures of the strength and direction
  of relationships).
— Bivariate (two factor) or multivariate (several or many factors) regression analysis (explaining instability with one or
  more 'predictive' determinants); and
— 'Causal' modeling ('maps' of complex relationships which
  explicitly recognize and test for 'causal' paths among the
  various factors).

A simple but plausible hypothesis to test is that current
instability reflects past instability. This *persistence* idea has
been tested in a number of studies in the form of historical
conflict traditions or the culture of violence concept, the idea
that past experience with violence makes the resort to violence
likely in the current situation. Lichbach and Gurr (1981)
developed and tested a formal model of this process. They view
internal conflict in terms of the two dimensions of protest
and rebellion and focus on both the extent (man-days of
participation) and intensity (number of deaths) of these two
types of internal conflict. In a test involving eighty-six nations
and the time period 1961–70, they discovered that:

— The simple persistence of conflict model holds much more
  for rebellion than for protest and for intensity more than
  extent.
— The shorter the time lag, the stronger the relationship (over

longer periods, the conflict persistence tendency becomes much weaker).

— *The fact that the 'conflict breeds conflict' assumption explains the intensity of a regime's response better than the extent of the challenger's actions justifies the emphasis in instability research on 'why people rebel' rather than 'why regimes repress.'*

The Lichbach and Gurr (1981) persistence model is a simple one, as they clearly recognize (in fact, they use it as a sort of baseline to compare with their more sophisticated work). Other research which looks at internal determinants of instability considers a host of potential causal factors. For example, quite a bit of research has been conducted on *economic sources of instability*. Zimmermann (1980) provides a good overview of the research in the area of political protest. Our discussion will include *short-term economic change, the overall level of economic development, the rate of growth, and socio-economic inequality*. Fenmore and Volgy (1978) deal with short-term economic change and political instability in seventeen Latin American countries between 1959 and 1967. Overall, thirty-nine of their fifty predicted relationships are supported. Short-term changes turn out to be important predictors of both political protest and elite instability. However, the pattern of political reactions to economic change depends on the nation's modernization level and type of government. In general, exports and the impact of the international economic environment have more influence than the level of domestic economic performance.

Zimmermann (1980) notes that much of the research on overall economic development supports the idea that lack of development is associated with high instability. Several studies, however, report that instability is highest at medium levels of development, suggesting that protest does not level off as a system becomes more developed. Modernization theory has popularized the idea that socio-economic development produces stable, democratic systems. Among many others (for example, Merkl 1981), Geller (1982) questions this idea. He analyzes twenty-one Latin American countries (1965–75) in order to test the hypothesis that bureaucratic authoritarianism is often the response to problems which surface at a fairly advanced stage in the development process. Modernization in Latin America politicizes new groups and sharply increases the overall level of politicization without necessarily providing institutions to mediate or limit this increased political activity. At the same time, economic crises—especially inflation—erupt. The net result is often a bureaucratic–authoritarian regime which tries to limit participation and eliminate spontaneous activity. Geller (1982) constructs and tests a causal model of the process: economic development leads to social mobilization,[8] which in turn is associated with political and economic crisis. Economic crisis seems to trigger the 'closing' of the political system. On the positive side:

— Geller's (1982) model 'works' in a statistical sense (for example, a lot of the potential variance—a measure of any statistical model's performance–is explained).
— Causal analysis traces a web of relationships and is therefore much more realistic and valid than simple correlation analysis.
— The indicators used to represent the concepts are unusually well selected and tap the phenomena very well.

Yet, there are a couple of serious problems:

— As Geller (1982) notes, future research must be pursued to specify the details and dynamics of the development-crisis-instability patterns.
— *There is a need to see if the findings hold up extensively (across time and cases) and intensively (in detailed case studies and comparative case studies), which is a recurring problem in comparative quantitative research.*

Change or rate of economic growth

This is another economic aspect which has received some attention. Olson (1963) reasoned that rapid economic change would bring about social dislocation and therefore instability, a prediction that is completely consistent with Durkheim. Rate of economic growth does seem to have a modest direct impact on instability (Hibbs 1973), with low rates of growth associated with higher levels of instability. When we look at all of the available evidence, however, the general conclusion seems to be that growth rates and instability do not have a simple, direct relationship (Eckstein 1980). Zimmermann (1980) points out that:

- The relationship may be negative in developed nations (with high growth associated with low instability) and positive in the Third World (with high growth associated with high instability).
- Such change may benefit some groups within a country and not others, but the research has concentrated on overall relationships.
- As in so many other quantitative explanatory efforts, the research has focused on a single point in time: what about patterns across time?

Socio-economic inequality

This has been examined in various studies as a determinant of instability. Russett (1964) finds that inequality of land owner-ship is related to high levels of instability. Sigelman and Simpson (1977) use personal income data and discover a little support for the idea that high inequality goes with high instability. In a refined test using two inequality data sets and two measures of political instability, Weede (1981) reports that high average income depresses political instability, but inequality shows little relationship to instability. Midlarsky (1982) revisits the inequality hypothesis, using as his point of departure the findings that land inequality turns out to be a potent predictor of mass revolution in agrarian societies. In such societies there is a tendency for the pattern of holdings to become more unequal with each new generation. An identical pattern of population growth and unequal landholdings characterized both France and Russia prior to their revolutions. Midlarsky speculates that the inequality conditions of late industrial developed societies may begin to resemble those of the agrarian sector, with equality of opportunity down and an increased division of labor (with inequality therefore possibly up). *Interestingly, for six highly industrialized societies, income inequalities have been increasing.* The United States has recently experienced an aver-age increase of 0.26 inequality units per year (while an indus-trializing Third World country like Taiwan has a recent record of average *decreases* of 1.5 units per year).

Overall, the Midlarsky (1982) study is significant in several respects:

- The empirical findings are strongly supported.
- Attention is given to a possible determinant of upheaval (and maybe revolution) in advanced societies.
- The evidence is based on both statistical and case study results, thereby appreciably increasing our confidence in its validity.

Structural imbalances

Societal theories attribute political instability to *societal processes*. According to societal theorists like Johnson (1966), society is a system which is 'normally' in a state of equilibrium. Political instability represents an abnormal force which disturbs the system's equilibrium. Tilly (1978) characterizes Johnson's theory in *Revolutionary Change* as a sequence of rapid change (which challenges the system), disequilibrium, overtaxed equilibrium mechanisms, individual disorientation, and protest. Some researchers in this tradition also consider divisions or cleavages in society. Not surprisingly, as cleavages increase, so does instability (Zimmermann 1980). Hibbs (1973) presents the most detailed and comprehensive analysis of social-cultural differences within a society. He considers both ethnic-linguistic diversity (a static or latent difference) and political separatism and group discrimination (active differences), testing the hypothesis that causal sequence is from the first to the second and then to political instability (especially in the case of more serious internal wars or rebellions).

Within the societal theory tradition, *structural imbalances* are said to exist when one aspect of development is high and the other low. For example, urbanization could be greater than the level of economic development, or educational levels could be higher than economic development. Both imbalances exist in many developing societies. The basic idea is that the imbalances lead to societal stress, individual dissatisfaction, and then political instability. In contrast, fully developed societies have balanced institutions and are appropriately 'stable.' But Hibbs (1973) tests the major imbalance hypotheses and finds strong support for none of them.

Samuel Huntington (1968) believes that *modernization causes instability*. The idea is very similar to Johnson's (1966): rapid social change leads to strain and therefore to instability. Huntington views society as a network of subsystems; developing countries experiencing modernization lack balance across at least some of their subsystems. Since institutions lag behind social and economic change, rapid social mobilizaton produces all kinds of dislocations, disorientation, and rising expectations. The strains which come with rapid mobilization generate increased political demands, which are destabilizing if the government lacks the capacity to handle the demands. As Huntington (1968: 47) expresses it:

Urbanization, increases in literacy, education, and media exposure [the determinants of social mobilization] all give rise to enhanced aspirations and expectations which, if unsatisfied, galvanize individuals and groups into politics. In the absence of strong and adaptable political institutions, such increases in participation mean instability and violence.

Sigelman's (1979) careful critique of Huntington's theory demonstrates that the theory is deceptively simple, imprecise, and possibly empirically wrong. Regarding the first charge, Huntington reduces his theory to three 'simple' formulae:

$$\frac{\text{Social Mobilization}}{\text{Economic Development}} = \text{Social Frustration}$$

$$\frac{\text{Social Frustration}}{\text{Mobility Opportunities}} = \text{Political Participation}$$

$$\frac{\text{Political Participation}}{\text{Political Institutionalization}} = \text{Political Instability}$$

Sigelman (1979) shows that the simplicity is deceptive. The first link—that mobilization leads to rising expectations and thereby to frustrations if the society is not affluent—actually conceals eight different assumptions and hypotheses. The concepts themselves are very imprecise. What is social mobilization? Is it a single dimension? What are the indicators of institutionalization? Measures of social frustration and mobility opportunities have not been developed. Finally, Sigelman (1979) reviews eight separate tests of the theory (all of which concern the gap between mobilization and institutionalization, with mobilization actually substituted for participation). The findings vary tremendously. Institutionalization turns out to be related to instability levels, but the results have been decidely mixed with respect to the effects of mobilization and the impact of the mobilization-institutionalization gap.

What can we conclude about the societal theories of instability? The critics have been less than enthralled. Among the overall conclusions are the following:

— It is impossible to find a direct, valid measure for the concept of equilibrium (Goldstone 1980).
— There is no way to know whether the reactions to change were adequate *before* the instability occurs (Tilly 1975).
— For the theory to hold, Durkheim's contention that individual pathology (suicide, crime, personal violence) and violent collective action are all related must hold. For 89 Italian provinces in the 1950s, there is evidence linking crime and public support for political extremism to the same general factors of socio-economic development (McHale 1978). Overall, however, Eckstein (1980) concludes that the evidence on this point is confusing.
— There is evidence that violent collective action is neither inherently 'non-routine' nor 'deviant,' contrary to Durkheim and his twentieth-century successors (Tilly 1978).
— The research has been primarily the kind that looks at many countries at one point in time, hardly an adequate way to study the impact of change and development.
— The concern is with societal conditions as they influence individuals and groups, but the evidence has been limited to measures taken from the level of societies.
— The process which intervenes between societal conditions and instability has been totally ignored (Aya 1979).
— Society is the central concept in this theory, but a state (with its structure of power relations and patterns of group conflicts) is not the same as a society (Aya 1979).

In addition to economic development and the balance between and among various elements of socio-economic development, there has also been explanatory *research on political development*. Hibbs (1973) tries to look systematically at the impact of political development on political violence. He includes indicators of democratic political development and a measure of whether or not the country has a communist regime. Being a democracy does not lower protest, but it does tend to reduce the extent of rebellion. Having a communist regime deflates collective protest and particularly reduces the amount of rebellion. Hibbs (1973) also analyzes the effect of the size of communist party membership in non-communist countries. This factor is fairly strongly associated with the level of protest (high membership/high protest) but not with rebellion.

Gurr (1974b) also focuses on type of political system, but in a much more basic and longer-term fashion. His concern is with the *durability* of political systems, defined in terms of persistence (how long the system exists) and adaptability (how well the system responds to the need for changes). *He does not find that durability is greater in countries where the political system is high in what he calls directiveness (defined basically as the scope of government) and complexity (of the decision-making institutions), thereby failing to find support for Huntington's thesis that institutionalization promotes stability. Nor do democratic traits guarantee durability.* What does matter is that systems with *consistently* democratic or authoritarian traits tend to persist—as opposed to systems marked by a lack of institutionalization. Gurr's data base consists of over 300 political systems in ninety-one countries from 1800 to 1971.

So what can we say about type of political system and instability? Gurr's study is valuable because it takes the long view and deals with basic stability. But the following points need to be raised:

— Gurr (1974b) excludes countries which became independent after 1945.
— Others have amended the results somewhat. Hannan and Carroll (1981) looked at ninety countries from 1950 to 1975 and discovered that per capita GNP, population, and ethnic diversity are the major determinants of overall rates of political change. Harmel (1980) undertook two re-analyses with less inclusive definitions of system-transforming change and found less support for the idea that durability of the system is greatest when authority traits are coherent or consistently democratic or authoritarian. 'Incoherent' (mixed trait) states which adapt in any direction proved to last longer than non-changing systems and lasted as long as systems with coherent patterns of authority. *These two studies reflect the common tendency in quantitative explanatory*

research for substantive results to change or become quali-
fied if different definitions are used (Harmel 1980) or
different slices of time are selected (Hannan and Carroll
1981).
- Long-term system survival is clearly important, but this kind
  of approach excludes less dramatic forms of instability.
- Political development or type of political system is an important factor for analyzing instability in a very fundamental
  way. Even if we restrict the focus to developing countries or
  'LDCs,' generalizations often do not hold up across types.
  Hibbs (1973) includes most countries in his causal model;
  Sanders (1978) re-analyzed the data by looking at different
  regions of the world and found that different groups of
  countries show very different patterns.[9] *Much of the quanti-*
  tative explanatory research compares all or most countries
  at once; we offer a note of caution about interpreting these
  results too uncritically if the researcher has not broken the
  countries down into types or regional clusters.

The interest in different types of political systems reminds
us of the importance of persistence and the role of both the
performance of the system and its perceived legitimacy. A system
which always performed superbly would be expected to be high
in legitimacy and would persist. A system which failed miser-
ably would lack legitimacy and would therefore be a prime
candidate for extinction or fundamental system change. In the
real world, things are rarely neat, however. Lipset (1960)
demonstrates that there are different ways to combine system
effectiveness and legitimacy. Some systems may be 'effective'
but not legitimate in the eyes of its people. Other systems may
not be performing well but may persist because of past successes
and a reservoir of legitimacy (some Western democracies in the
1930s) or because of symbols which promote legitimacy and the
effects of aspirations for the future (Mexico after its revolution in the early 1900s). In addition, rulers in all political
systems rely on force or coercion as the ultimate weapon to
assure system persistence. This is true of democratic as well as
authoritarian nations. A very ineffective system—one that is
not producing policies that satisfy its people or 'outputs' that
keep them happy—may persist despite low effectiveness and
lack of legitimacy.

Zimmermann's (1979a) basic model of internal crisis incorporates coercion into a performance–legitimacy–persistence model. High coercion and performance both impact upon legitimacy, which in turn determines persistence along with coercion, performance, and violence. But political violence ultimately receives all of the direct and indirect impact from performance, legitimacy, coercion, and persistence.

Zimmermann's model is procedural and basically causal, though the formality of a statistical causal model is not presented here. Internal political violence is conceived as the 'dependent variable,' while coercion, performance, legitimacy, and persistence are conceived as 'independent variables,' though not directly since some of the variables impact upon others in the causal chain.

Jacobson (1973a) tries to test an instability theory which incorporates legitimacy, performance (effectiveness), and coerciveness. Using data from a variety of sources, he focuses on but three primary sets of factors. His variables are by no means comprehensive, though they are designed to measure a number of specific phenomena. In any case, the three sets are presented below.

— demands and support from the population (demands for government action and expressions of support for the government);
— characteristics of the government (complexity, coerciveness, and performance); and
— conflict or instability (Gurr's indicators of turmoil, conspiracy, and internal war).

He also treats public demands and support (legitimacy) and characteristics of the government (including performance) as independent or causal factors which influence the amount of political instability. Demands and support affect instability directly as well as indirectly (through their impact on the government). His indicators for the independent factors are very crude and indirect. For example, he uses three indicators to measure support or legitimacy: a rating of government stability; the number of deaths due to domestic group violence; and the number of executive turnovers. Overall, the results are decent but far from spectacular, although the model works pretty well for explaining instability in developed societies when he breaks the test down into traditional, modernizing, and developed countries.

In a simpler but more interesting model, Heggen and Cuzan (1981) analyze legitimacy, coercion, and scope (the extent of government control over societal resources) for five Central American countries and Cuba in the late 1960s and early 1970s. The basic idea is an analogy between government and an economic firm. An efficient government is one which reaches a level of scope by selecting a mix of coercion and legitimacy which minimizes the total cost to the government. In the short-run, the cost for extra coercion is low; higher legitimacy is expensive (if not impossible). But in the long run, the social costs of legitimacy are much lower than those of coercion.

Heggen and Cuzan (1981) define scope as the percentage of GDP (Gross Domestic Product) consumed by the government. For coercion, they use the measure of the ratio of military personnel per 1,000. For legitimacy, the overall status of democracy or electoral competition is the indicator. In their study, Nicaragua showed very little change during the 1960s and early 1970s in its coercion–legitimacy balance. In Nicaragua, coercion decreased but both legitimacy and scope remained constant.[10] El Salvador, Guatemala, and Honduras were all low in legitimacy and became lower during the period. In Cost Rica, legitimacy went up. Cuba's high level of coercive power peaked in 1969 and remained high through 1974, while per capita GNP declined at an annual rate of 0.4 percent from 1960 to 1976.

One obvious way to measure legitimacy would be to ask the country's population. Very little good public opinion data are available, however, and we know very little about the relationship between people's attitudes and system persistence and change. Muller and Williams (1980) report results for an analysis of a sample of the public in West Germany. The people interviewed were asked about their support for or alienation from the political system and their satisfaction with the government's outputs in both 1974 and 1976. Support-alienation tapped the idea of legitimacy and output satisfaction measured their evaluation of the system's performance. Interestingly, quite a few individuals changed on the legitimacy scale from 1974 to 1976. With respect to the relationship between legitimacy and peformance evaluation, Muller and Williams (1980) uncovered evidence for two kinds of processes: change in legitimacy as a result of output satisfaction levels and legitimacy attitudes influencing performance evaluation. On the basis of their complex model tests, they concluded that performance evaluation and legitimacy attitudes may be interrelated, with the two 'causing' each other rather than legitimacy shaping attitudes about the system's performance. Other evidence about legitimacy and its relationship to behavior against the political system is available for New York City, urban Costa Rica, and Guadalajara, Mexico (Muller *et al.* 1982). In all three cases, people low in legitimacy support were engaged in aggressive political participation, but none of these studies takes measurements at more than one point in time.

Evaluations about the government's performance, attitudes about its legitimacy, and political stability or instability are undoubtedly related. Exactly how and to what extent, unfortunately, we do not know. This line of research can be evaluated with the following generalizations:

— Most of the studies use very *indirect* measures of legitimacy and very simple and inadequate measures of performance and coercion. We remain uncertain about the true relationships.
— Relevant public opinion data are available only for the United States and a few other countries. Even here, the amount is limited.
— The Booz-Allen (1981) report is correct in its emphasis on assets held by the regime and opposition groups and coalitions and also right in concluding that the minimum requirement for regime survival is a prevailing belief on the part of the population in some aspect of the regime's legitimacy. However, we know little about the dynamics and nature of the relationships among the key factors discussed above.
— The orientation leads to a shift in instability analysis from an exclusive concern with domestic instability *events* to an accompanying concern with domestic instability *situations* and *crises*.
— We know even less about instability *crises* than about general legitimacy–performance–persistence relationships. In general, however, these kinds of crises '. . . call for and possibly lead to *substantial* changes in policies or the political order, respectively, not to a mere replacement of personnel'

(Zimmermann, 1979a: 69; emphasis in the original; see also Verba, 1971).

We have now introduced a simple persistence model as well as approaches which consider a variety of economic, societal, and political system characteristics. The emphasis on performance and legitimacy moved us toward a concern with more dynamic and immediate determinants of instability. The internal political process approach, which draws heavily on Tilly's (1975, 1978) collective action theory (CAT), moves us even farther into the arena of day-to-day politics and concrete political actors and processes.[11]

Aya (1979) charges that Durkheim, Chalmers Johnson, Samuel Huntington, and other societal theorists (as well as many of the psychological studies on instability to be discussed soon) engage in a two-stage leap of faith. The first leap is from social change to the appearance of grievances that lead eventually to collective violence and the second is from these discontents to political action. In neither instance is the actual process explained.

The *origins* of collective violence and revolution are in the structure and workings of politics, not in rage or other emotions, which may go along with collective activity of this nature but do not *cause* it (Aya 1979). The CA approach is also referred to as the political science or pluralist-interest group approach, although many political scientists use other approaches and many of its advocates are not political scientists. In Tilly's (1978) version of the theory, the basic concept is the group. The central focus is the interaction of groups in the political process. Tilly develops a 'polity model,' which consists of a population, a government, one or more contenders (members of the system and/or challengers), a polity, and coalitions. He also offers a mobilization model, where the analysis revolves around the concepts of interests, organizations, mobilization, and collective action or CA. The extent of CA is the product of a group's power, its mobilization, and the current opportunities and threats confronting its interests. The group's power and/or the amount of repression directed at the group determine the opportunities available for CA. Tilly (1978) analyzes CA by using a variety of quantitative measures (although a case study or qualitative approach would also be feasible). He maintains that violent events can serve as useful tracers of general CA trends. A full test of the model involves the measurement of interests, organization, and mobilization (as well as power, opportunity/threat, and repression).

Most of these concepts are very elusive when it comes to measurement. Interests, for example, can be inferred from the attitudes and actions of the population or from analysis of the presumed links beween interest and social action; but as Tilly (1978) readily admits, neither alternative is ideal. Organization refers to people who share characteristics and interact actively. One feasible way to generate a list of all potential groups would be to use divisions within the electorate or labor force, but the measurement of internal networks is very difficult. It is also hard to measure mobilization; Tilly offers two possible but very imperfect strategies. Power measurement is the most elusive of all.

Tilly's empirical research sketches forms of CA across time, examines violent CA (our definition of political instability), and then builds on Tilly (1975) to consider 'extreme' or crisis CA (revolution and rebellion). In general, he distinguishes among competitive, reactive, and proactive group claims. Tilly surveys Western Europe and North America from 1400 to the present, noting the changing trends across time. Groups losing power are exemplified by peasant rebellions (tax rebellions, food riots). New group rights ignited a series of strikes, demonstrations, and other challenging events in the late 1800s and the 1900s. Collective violence, according to Tilly, grows out of interactions among groups. CA violence often involves new contenders and declining members and therefore tends to cluster around entries into and exits from politics. Tilly also defines a revolutionary situation as one of 'multiple sovereignty,' with more than one bloc effectively controlling a significant part of the national machinery. There are three immediate causes of revolutionary situations for Tilly:

— The appearance of contenders who advance exclusive and alternative claims to control over the government (signalled by the outpouring of new ideologies with goals that are incompatible with the continued existence of the current regime).
— A significant part of the population shows commitment to

the new claims (especially when the government suddenly fails to meet its obligations or unexpectedly imposes new ones).
— Government agents are unable (or unwilling) to suppress the alternative coalition (often because of a sudden change in the balance of coercive resources, because of the loss of a war or foreign intervention).

Tilly (1978) avoids the social movement as a concept for analyzing CA. We feel, however, that social movements are often integrally involved in the causes and processes associated with political instability. McCarthy and Zald (1977) offer a theory of social movements and resource mobilization which is stated in terms of Tilly's interest group/political process theory. They regard social movements as preferences for social change of various kinds and distinguish between social movements (general interests), social movement organizations (formal organizations), the social movement industry (all movements in a given area, such as the civil rights 'industry'), and the entire social movement sector of society (all 'industries'). Of particular value is the economic model they use for analyzing competition among social movement organizations. Organization goals can be viewed as products and supporters can be seen as consumers with a demand for products. Some useful hypotheses are developed out of the economic firm analogy. For example, movements dependent on isolated members rather than chapter organizations will devote more resources to advertising. Movement organizers can be regarded as entrepreneurs. In some cases, then, demand may be reinforced, channelled, or even created. McCarthy and Zald (1977) reject the idea that shared grievances and general beliefs about group action invariably lead to movements. Movements may arise to crystallize and convert beliefs into action (or create shared beliefs), thus reversing the grievances-movement chain of causation. We would add movements to Tilly's category of organizations. For instability analysis, we may want to think about developing different models for social movements as opposed to other types of organizations.

Instability theories which highlight groups and the internal political process feature a number of strengths and weaknesses:

— Collective violence approaches center on the important question of how violence occurs rather than just why.

— The group approach does not have to exclude other factors. Overholt's (1977) organizational conflict theory of revolution explicitly advocates the analysis of other factors (participants, leaders, ideologies, more remote causes, etc.) through their impact on the revolutionary group and the government group.
— Much of the support is indirect. For example, evidence that collective violence is not more likely in periods of rapid change weakens a competing theory but does not directly support collective action theory (Snyder 1978).
— How to measure the critical factor in the theory—the magnitude of interest group conflict—is a very big and unanswered question (Goldstone 1980).
— Data problems are massive and perhaps insurmountable.
— The theory may be insufficient alone; it excludes both the initial preconditions of and the historical context for instability.
— It may be necessary to combine the internal politics and another theory to explain instability adequately (Korpi 1974).
— When the theory is confronted with the relative deprivation theory, its main 'competitor,' the results have been mixed, weak, and confusing (Eckstein 1980; Snyder 1978).

What we call the *'psychological-aggregate' approach to explaining political instability* concentrates on individuals and factors at that level but implicitly or explicitly combines their attitudes and beliefs into an 'aggregate.' The basic premise here is that individual feelings and perceptions are a primary cause of instability. In the most popular version of this theory, 'relative deprivation' is advanced as the major determinant of instability (Davies 1962, 1969; Feierabend and Feierabend 1966, 1972; Gurr 1968a, 1968b, 1970; Feierabend *et al.* 1972). Our overview relies on Muller's (1980) comprehensive review of research in this area. Initially, however, we should stress that it is especially important to look at the incentives that operate at the individual level in terms of participation in movements. Roeder (1982) tests the by-product theory of revolutionary involvement, which states that involvement in revolutionary movements is often a by-product of participation in the movement which has other, personal, non-revolutionary functions for the individual. (The actual test concerns peasant revolutionary activity in Russia prior to 1917.) It is important to keep this in mind as we survey the many studies which rely on a theory of psychological determinants of collective behavior but do not really use individual data. What the relevant individual beliefs and needs are and what impact they have are both open questions at this point. Critiques which ridicule psychological theories of instability completely and conveniently gloss over this very important fact (for example, Aya 1979). The various theorists in this school trace the roots of revolution and other violent collective change to the state of mind of the masses. For James Davies (1962), the main source of revolution is a reaction to a short-term economic reversal following a long period of improvement. The Feierabends (1972) identify modernization as the culprit. Gurr (1970) zeroes in on the denial of political or economic opportunities to ethnic and/or other groups in a society. All of them converge in emphasizing the role of an intolerable gap between what people want and what they get as the crucial determinant of potential collective violence. For Gurr (1970), relative deprivation arises when an individual does not get what is seen as justifiably due to him or her—the just deserts form of relative deprivation.

There seems to be little or no relationship between actual or objective deprivation and collective violence (McPhail 1971). But relative deprivation refers to people's perceptions, not to actual conditions. You can be very poor but not revolutionary —abject poverty seems to predict to apathy more than anything else. You can be well off but very dissatisfied. What counts is your perception. In a study of the West German public in the early 1970s, Muller (1977, 1979) finds a moderately strong relationship between a just deserts measure of frustration and a scale measuring aggressive political participation (collective violence at the individual level). Other research —Muller's (1980) in New York City and Barnes et al. (1979) in Britain, the United States, Austria, Holland, and West Germany—finds almost no relationship between just deserts frustration and political protest potentials.

Muller and Jukam's (1983) study also reports a minimal relationship between variables measuring just deserts frustration and aggressive political participation in New York City public and university samples. Perceived rank disequilibrium (that is, a discrepancy between education and income/occupation, as in the 'intellectual proletariat' syndrome), another popular hypothesized precursor, also plays a role of minimal impact. Alienation is the key predictor variable in the models for both samples, although the overall performance of the 'best' models is far from spectacular.

Although aggregate and survey data have been the primary methodological vehicles for amassing information about relative deprivation, psychologists have also examined the phenomenon experimentally. Laboratory studies, as is well-known, suffer from limits to external validity, or the inability to generalize with confidence to the real world. However, such research is valuable because of its ability to illuminate fundamental causal relationships while extraneous factors are held constant; field studies seem to be more useful, but it is often overlooked that such research cannot easily disentangle complex relationships (internal validity is high in the laboratory, but low in the field).

Folger *et al.* (1983) furnish a particularly relevant example of relative deprivation and procedural justifications in an experiment on cognitions available to subjects about outcomes in the form of rewards. In an experiment with undergraduates involving a competitive situation, Folger *et al.* predict that hypothesized differences in discontent should surface only when inadequate justifications are offered for an unsatisfactory outcome, not when extensive and procedural justifications are provided. This should qualify the tendency for discontent to result more from a procedural change where the old procedure would have yielded better outcomes than the new one (as opposed to a condition involving outcomes that are no better under the new procedure). Resentment, they infer, may not materialize if sufficient reasons are given to account for why the actual outcomes fall short of those desired (e.g., public satisfaction with economic adversity if such conditions are plausibly justified in terms of the nation's long-term good).

Many of the relative deprivation studies, it should be emphasized, operationalize egoistic or personal relative deprivation. Guimond and Dubé-Simard (1983), in contrast, focus on fraternal relative deprivation (see also Rhodebeck (1981)), on the somewhat similar concept of group deprivation). In a questionnaire study of Francophones in Montreal, Quebec,

Guimond and Dubé-Simard look at group-to-group rather than individual-to-group comparisons. The feeling of fraternal relative deprivation turns out to be as strongly related to a general index of Francophone nationalism as the perceived economic gap between the two groups for eighty Francophone respondents. In contrast, measures of egoistic relative deprivation or personal discontent are not related to this index.

Fraternal relative deprivation thus emerges as a more important probable precursor of protest movements (and political instability generally) than the egoistic variant. This interpretation certainly dovetails with the extensive empirical evidence about revolution and instability processes (e.g., the emphasis in the literature on ethnicity as a source of protest and violence, the work on peasants and other classes and strata, and the more general theories of social movements and collective action) and suggest that relative deprivation ought to be nominated for 'rehabilitation' as an explanatory concept in instability research.

Gurr (1970) argues that feelings about the justification for or against violence could increase or decrease the effects of just deserts frustration. Utilitarian justification refers to whether or not political violence is perceived to be useful. Normative justification involves the belief that violence *should* be used. Muller's (1979) measure of normative justification combines political alienation with the degree of commitment to an ideological position that approves of political aggression (leftism in the West German context). In addition to utilitarian justification and personal normative beliefs, social normative beliefs—whether or not the individual was in a university and therefore received special support for political aggression—are also included. His model, which includes these and several other factors, peforms quite well in accounting for West German attitudes about aggressive political participation. Muller (1980: 97) concludes his review by pointing to the strong support for justification beliefs as determinants of potential political violence: 'people rebel when they believe it is right to rebel and that rebellion will pay off.'

People may participate in politics in a democratic or aggressive fashion (Muller 1977, 1979). Muller (1982) develops an integrated model of democratic and aggressive participation for his West German data set. He discovers that 'political efficacy' (feelings of competence as a citizen) and psychological involvement in politics account for democratic participation. Aggressive participation is another cause of democratic participation. A low sense of efficacy and high psychological involvement are associated with aggressive participation (if the individual also feels that aggressive participation has a good chance of success). There is a fairly strong tendency for individuals who engage in aggressive participation to expand their behavior to include democratic participation at a later point. This finding also has implications for theories of political instability. It provides support for the argument that stability and instability are points on a continuum and that aggressive participation or violent collective action is not necessarily or invariably a pathological form of behaviour or an activity of only the uprooted and disorientated.

Efficacy is looked at more directly in Sigelman and Feldman's (1983) test of the 'mistrustful-efficacious' hypothesis—the idea that low political trust and high efficacy are an explosive combination likely to lead to aggressive political mobilization. They review the many previous empirical analyses in this area, cataloging their many shortcomings. Sigelman and Feldman employ data from the eight-nation study of political action (Barnes *et al.* 1979) in Western Europe and the United States to test a series of models relating to mistrust (conceived as policy dissatisfaction rather than generic mistrust) and feelings of subjective competence or efficacy.

Generally, a simple additive model of the trust-efficacy variables predicts protest at least as successfully as the interactive form, which assumes that it is the *combination* of low trust and high efficacy that is crucial, not the independent contributions of each. The addition of three exogenous variables —age, use of ideology, and anti-establishment orientation—not surprisingly improves the empirical performance of the model rather dramatically; again, the multiplicative versus additive form does not seem to matter very much.

To what extent is political instability the product of people's beliefs, attitudes, and other perceptions and feelings? Aya (1979), Tilly (1975, 1978) and others have been sharply critical of research directed at such questions. So are we, but for different reasons. We do not doubt the basic utility of work on mass psychological characteristics for explaining instability ,[12] but we have very real reservations about the way it has been done so far. Our critique includes the following points:

- Many of the early studies did not measure individual charac-teristics but used indicators at the national level to 'represent' individual perceptions and attitudes. This is the kind of 'representation' that even Edmund Burke would look down upon. It leads nowhere and says nothing of value about the impact of mass discontent or beliefs.
- The available research which does take into account individual attitudes and beliefs is limited to Western democracies; caution about generalizing to other types of nations is very much in order.
- *Which* individual characteristics determine the potential for participation in collective violence?
- What are the determinants of beliefs and other individual characteristics which affect collective violence?
- We would also recommend against throwing relative depri-vation out prematurely. In at least certain situations, socially shared deprivation might be a critical factor. In addition to Guimond and Dubé-Simard (1983), Dibble (1981) reaches this conclusion in her re-analysis of data on black Americans gathered for the Kerner Commission. She finds that an individual's experience of deprivation is not strongly related to support for violence unless it is shared with others.
- Individual characteristics are preconditions and say nothing about the process of instability—how frustrations are changed into collective action of any kind.
- Some of the psychological approaches have ignored non-psychological factors and have therefore been simplistic. This is true of Davies as well as the Feierabends.
- Aside from Muller's research, which used data from the same people in West Germany in 1974 and 1976, the psychological studies have been overwhelmingly anchored to one point in time. The effects of long-run changes in deprivation or beliefs therefore have to be judged by the unsatisfactory strategy of comparing countries at a single point in time, rather than by following trends across time (Tilly 1975).
- Collective violence against the state has been the main concern. State use of violence has often been ignored and collective violence *between* contenders for power has not been studied at all in these analyses.
- The Tilly theory has been set up as an opponent of the

psychological theories. Eckstein's (1980) assessment of the evidence indicates that there is a lot of ambiguity and neither one really 'wins.' Maybe we should start to think about combining the two approaches rather than continuing to engage in pointless debates about them.

— If we really did want to test the internal politics-group theory against the relative deprivation and related theories, we would need data about groups, individuals, and their links (Snyder 1978), but such data do not exist except for very small groups and limited situations.

Political elites represent the final category in the list of intranational determinants of political instability. What elites say and do has an impact on collective action of both the non-violent and violent kinds. How elites manage instability crises has some relevance to their final outcomes. Although Goldstone (1980: 433) is fundamentally correct in concluding that elite action may not be able to forestall revolutions, state rulers are not merely passive victims of 'structural' forces beyond their control. They are also considerably less constrained in non-revolutionary collective violence situations. Furthermore, the jury is still out on the question of 'voluntarist' versus 'deterministic' theories of revolutions. We lean toward the viewpoint that both are relevant to explaining instability. To an extent, the choice depends upon how you look at the problem. Eckstein (1980) discusses this in the context of the distinction between the contingency theory (the normal state of society is peace and collective violence is an aberration) and the inherency theory (violence is inherent and to be expected). Contingency theory leads to a concern with feelings and emotions, which can range from deprivation and relative deprivation (Gurr 1970) to a sense of indignation about poverty and injustice (Scott 1977; Lupsha 1971). Inherency theory assumes that the potential for collective violence is always there and that cost–benefit calculations predominate, leading to violence in some instances and non-violence in others. Our definition of instability as any form of collective political violence favors the inherency theory, but we would incorporate anger, frustration, and a lot of other beliefs and perceptions into any genuine 'theory' of political instability.

The rulers of the government are also important actors in Tilly's group-collective action theory. Elites are active participants in political instability processes and are much more than neutral umpires as they repress some groups and facilitate the activities of others (Tilly 1978). In Gurr's (1970) theory, the elite factor enters primarily through the balance between the regime and the opposition, one of the forces which mediates (lessens or increases) the importance of relative deprivation. Elites are also of vital importance in theories which emphasize performance, legitimacy, and coercion:

— both protest and rebellion evoke elite repression;
— a key causal pattern flows from protest, to repression, and then to rebellion;
— rebellion, coups, and repression are interrelated; and
— in the short run, repression elicits more violence. In the long run, it deters rebellion but not protest.

Zimmermann (1980) summarizes the research on elite coercion, concluding (1) that elite coercive capability is not strongly related to the amount of protest that occurs, (2) neither capability nor its use deters conflict, and (3) the actual use of force seems to increase collective violence. The patterns probably differ, however, according to the type of nation and form of conflict.

We distinguish between coups, which involve the elite or an elite counter-elite, and collective violence (although the two may certainly affect each other). O'Kane (1981) attempts to explain the occurrence of coups by testing a model which involves several basic causes (poverty, economic specialization, and the export of primary goods) and several obstacles (recent independence, whether a previous coup has taken place, and the presence of foreign troops). Overall, the results support the hypotheses about the causes of and obstacles to coups in 125 countries for the period 1950–70. O'Kane uses discriminant analysis, a statistical technique similar to regression analysis, which is used when the factor to be explained is a yes–no situation (a coup occurred or did not). Discriminant analysis classifies the countries into categories on the basis of the factors used to explain the outcome—the causes or stimulants of coups and the obstacles. Only four countries are wrongly classified in the sense that a coup occurred but was not statistically predicted.

In 18 nations, a coup was predicted but had not occurred as of 1970. Since then, nine of the 18 have experienced coups and several more have had attempted coups. O'Kane also examines the results if the obstacles of foreign troops were removed, with the interesting result that the Philippines and five other countries were then 'predicted' to have coups. O'Kane (1981) attributes coups to unstable and sometimes hopeless economic situations. Jackman (1978) combines political and social factors in an analysis of the determinants of coups in black African nations from 1960 through 1975. The results include the following:

— Both social mobilization (measured by the percentage of the labor force in non-agricultural occupations plus the literacy level) and the presence of a dominant cthnic group produce coups.
— Multi-partyism promotes coups while electoral turnout (in the last election prior to the country's independence) makes them less likely.
— Multi-partyism is especially likely to lead to coups if there is a dominant ethnic group.
— If turnout is high, multi-partyism's effect on coups disappears.

Overall, the model performs extremely well in explaining coups.

Zimmermann (1979b, 1979c) tries to develop a much more complete and complex causal model for explaining *coups d'état*. He asserts that characteristics of both the military and the society are probably important for explaining coups. Military grievances and factionalism, regime vulnerability and its possible causes, internal war, external war, and past coups are among the specific factors identified. However, the model has not actually been tested and is a map for the future rather than a source of reliable findings at this point.

O'Kane (1983) attempts to test an array of theories about the determinants of coups via cross-sectional multiple regression models for 1968, with coups operationalized dichotomously as a dummy dependent variable (a coup occurred or did not occur, 1950–71). She considers theoretical perspectives which view coups as: agents of modernization; the outcomes of social cleavages; consequences of economic dependence; and the outcomes of correctly calculated strategies.

Statistically, the findings are extremely weak, except for one model which ends up consisting of two statistically significant explanatory variables (previous occurrence of a coup and defense expenditures as a percentage of the budget). However, the jury is really still out on this; the model specifications and variable operationalization strategies are uniformly simplistic, and there is a marked overreliance on crude and readily available single variables rather than composite indicators for complex concepts. (In contrast, in the area of general instability research, Sanders (1981) provides a textbook example of how to proceed with model specification, and Gurr and Lichbach (1979) furnish an equally exemplary tutorial for developing composite indicators for complex constructs.)

Aside from repression and coups, elite factors include the attitudes and belief systems and other personal characteristics of both elites in power and potential elites. Potential elites, such as the leaders of revolutionary movements, generally differ considerably from their followers (Greene 1974). They are often of much higher status and better educated. The role of intellectuals in revolutions has also received a considerable amount of attention. The special contributions of Lenin, Trotsky, Mao, Castro, and other revolutionary leaders have been documented in numerous studies.

Potential leaders and intellectuals articulate and propagate revolutionary ideologies, which explain discontent, justify action, recommend conflict strategies, identify key targets of revolutionary action, and provide tools for mobilizing the masses and manipulating support from crucial groups in society (Overholt 1977). Elite-based armed revolutionary parties are singled out as the indispensable source of peasant mobilization in some accounts (Migdal 1974). Russell (1974) and many others demonstrate that military elites can be equally crucial —revolution is impossible when the armed forces are united and effectively employed. Overall, we know very little about the psychological dynamics and other characteristics of revolutionary elites (Rejai 1980).

Approaches used to analyze actual and potential political elites are also applicable to *the study of terrorism*. Terrorism may be used as part of a collective violence strategy, although extensive collective violence and terrorism are not particularly compatible.[13] Generally, terrorism is really a weapon of the weak—and of those who lack a mass base. For the analysis of elite terrorist sects, it probably makes sense to adapt the approaches, methods, and techniques which have been used in the study of political elites. For example, various analytical methodologies have been used in a fairly productive fashion to explain the decisions of foreign policy-makers. These methods and techniques, which have been borrowed from cognitive and social psychology, are inventoried, evaluated, and illustrated with respect to foreign policy elites in Hopple (1980b) and elsewhere.

Crenshaw's (1981) essay, which deals with the causes of terrorism, supports this recommendation. Terrorism has been attributed to a wide range of causes, including some rather fanciful theories of individual psychopathology and a variety of highly specific explanations. Crenshaw discusses the more systematic causal factors and focuses on the setting or pre-conditions for terrorism, the processes of terrorism, and its social and political effects. Subsumed under the setting are a number of permissive factors, which set the stage by providing opportunities for terrorism. Modernization, urbanization, historical traditions of violence, and the transnational communication of terrorist ideologies are among the preconditions for terrorist activity.

The question of individual motivation and participation arises because terrorism 'is neither an automatic reaction to conditions nor a purely calculated strategy . . . terrorists are only a small minority of people with similar backgrounds, experiencing the same conditions' (Crenshaw 1981: 390). It therefore becomes imperative to look into personality factors and especially the beliefs and attitudes of terrorists.

Social psychology also enters into the picture in a major way because terrorism is usually a group activity, involving very close relations among a few people: 'Isolation and internal consensus explain how the beliefs and values of a terrorist group can be so drastically at odds with those of society at large . . . in their intense commitment, separation from the outside world, and intolerance of internal dissent, terrorist groups resemble religious sects or cults' (Crenshaw 1981: 393). Terrorism of the highly ideological small sect variety, therefore, can most profitably be analyzed as a problem of individual psychology (values, beliefs, motives and reasons, information processing and other aspects of judgment and choice) and social psychology (small group interactions, leader-follower relations, 'groupthink' and related processes).

We have now introduced an array of causes ,within a nation which could explain political instability. *Factors external to the nation must also be taken into consideration.* The French Revolution became an example for all potential revolutionaries, as did the Bolshevik and Chinese revolutions in the twentieth century. Castro's victory in Cuba set off a chain reaction in Latin America, although the success of his efforts was not duplicated elsewhere. More recently, the Sandinista victory in Nicaragua has provided a model for revolutionaries elsewhere in Central America. Economic and political relationships between nations also emerge as factors worthy of attention.

According to Kerbo (1978), external involvement in collective violence may be direct and intentional or indirect and unintentional. It may affect the preconditions leading to internal violence or the later stages. An example of unintentional, indirect foreign influence on the development of internal political violence is Paige's (1975) theory of political violence and export agriculture, which examines the impact of the world economic system and resulting forms of agriculture production. Situations in which an external nation unintentionally affects the later stages of political violence are also relevant (for example, the effects of Japan's invasion of China on Mao's eventual victory in the Chinese civil war). Gurr (1970) and others consider the most prominent intentional factor during the later stages: foreign support for the old regime or the rebels. The fourth category, where outsiders intentionally try to disrupt the country and create or reinforce the preconditions for instability, has been relatively neglected. Countries on the periphery of the world capitalist system may be expected to experience more of this fourth form of external involvement.

Kick (1980), drawing on the world systems approach, spells out the way in which external influences operate on domestic processes. The world system approach assumes that a capitalist world economy shapes much of the behavior of its member nations, which can be classifed into core, semi-periphery, and periphery states. Core states can directly manipulate the weak peripheral societies both economically and politically.

World   system   properties   affect   national   political   and economic characteristics directly and thereby influence political conflict. Foreign penetration may also determine patterns of political activity in periphery nations. Because of its more equal distribution of wealth, larger middle class, and so forth, the core state will experience less intense internal conflict. The periphery confronts fundamentally different structural conditions. As a result of world historical conditions, internal political and economic characteristics, and direct foreign interference, such nations are weaker and less able to deter attempts to overthrow the government. States in the periphery can expect more conflict of unlimited means (internal war) and unlimited ends (seizure of power).

Most of the quantitative research on external explanations of internal violence concerns either the contagion of violence or various forms of economic or political penetration. Contagion research rests on the premise that a demonstration effect may account for collective violence, just as consumers change their consumption patterns as they see their neighbors change (Greene 1974). Interestingly, revolutions, coups, and other forms of internal conflict and violence do not seem to be distributed randomly through history, but tend to cluster together. The American Revolution in the 1770s apparently set off a a chain reaction, with the French Revolution occurring in 1789, a series of revolutions in central and northern Europe, and then the Latin American independence movements. The Paris revolution of 1830 provided the impetus for a series of nationalistic and revolutionary movements in Poland, Belgium, and elsewhere. The 1848 uprising in Paris provided the context for a similar reaction throughout Europe. The Bolshevik revolution, which was followed by temporary Soviet-style governments in Hungary and Bavaria, served as a model for Mussolini and Hitler. Both the Bolshevik and Chinese revolutions have been examples for potential Marxist revolutionaries throughout the world.

Quite a few *quantitative analyses of contagion or diffusion* have also been undertaken. Pitcher et al. (1978) provide evidence for the temporal diffusion of collective violence in their work, using 25 data sets and 10 forms of collective violence. The idea that military coups spread in a contagion-like process has attracted a great deal of interest (Laemmle 1977; Li and Thompson 1975; Midlarsky 1970). Midlarsky (1978) finds evidence of contagion with respect to US urban riots in the

1960s, although the strength of the evidence has been questioned. Govea and West (1981) report limited evidence for riot contagion within Latin American countries between 1949 and 1963. Midlarsky *et al.* (1980) use the Rand terrorism data for 1968 to 1974 to test for the spread of international terrorism. Diffusion held from 1968 to 1971 and the evidence supported a contagion-as-direct-modeling process for 1973–74. Bombings, kidnappings, and—to a lesser extent—hijackings are more contagious than assassinations and riots.

Diffusion refers to the spread of a particular type of behavior as the result of the cumulative impact of a set of statistically independent events. Contagion is a direct modeling process where later behavior is a direct imitation of earlier behavior. This distinction is important. Midlarsky's (1978) analysis of US urban disorders in 1966–67 uncovers a diffusion pattern for larger cities, where each precipitant or immediate cause of the riot was an independent event involving interactions between blacks and the police, and a direct contagion effect for small cities, where riots occurred because of contagion from large cities. Similarly, Midlarsky *et al.* (1980) reason that Western European terrorists may have imitated Third World terrorists, with contagion rather than diffusion operating.

What is the evidence for diffusion or contagion as causes of collective violence? Several caveats must be noted:

— Most of the evidence refers to coups and terrorism. Both are primarily elite-based forms of behavior and therefore fall outside the scope of political instability defined as mass collective violence.
— There is some evidence that riots may spread within a country, although the available research does not permit us to be completely confident about this finding. However, diffusion or contagion (or both) may account for unplanned and unorganized collective violence.
— The diffusion or contagion of organized collective violence is not impossible and a lot of intuitive, anecdotal evidence suggests that successful revolutions set off chain-reactions and attract a number of imitators. However, we know nothing about the statistical strength of this tendency or how the process operates.
— Statistically, there is some disagreement about the best

or most appropriate ways to measure diffusion and contagion.

— Even if contagion seems to be the cause, the same conditions in the originating and the imitating countries may be the real cause (Zimmermann 1979c). It is very difficult to disentangle the internal preconditions from contagion processes.

— Contagion may play more of a role in explaining the *extent* of violence than the initial *causes* or *preconditions* (Govea and West 1981).

The *relationship between external and internal violence* has been the focus of a number of quantitative investigators. As Stohl (1980) points out in his review of this research, some of the efforts look at external and internal conflict and others consider the impact of war on internal violence. Ironically, internal-external conflict studies have proliferated since Rummel's (1963) finding that there is no apparent relationship between conflict within and between nations. One study reports that external conflict is negatively associated with internal conflict for nations that are highly militarized, which means that internal conflict increases when external conflict is down and vice versa. A few studies discover that both forms tend to go up and down together. Many uncover stronger relationships when specific types of nations and forms of conflict are investigated. Quite a few published analyses fail to find any noteworthy relationships. Many critiques of the quantitative internal conflict-external conflict literature have appeared. Scolnick (1974) reviews a number of problems related to data and methodology. Zimmermann (1980) catalogs a similar list (for example, source coverage problems) and offers a number of suggestions for improving future work. Mack (1975) hates everything about the research and rejects all of it in a wide-ranging attack which proceeds from data and methodological criticisms to concerns about theory and epistemology. But research which tries to blend case studies in a systematic and sequential fashion with quantitative research might yield some payoffs.[14] At the present time, however, what we have is a maze of conflicting and confusing findings. Overall, the research has consumed a lot of computer output paper but produced little of real value:

— The various studies differ in so many ways (time periods, ways of combining the data, basic analytical methods, and so forth) that the effects of varying research methods preclude definitive generalizations and make it impossible to unearth substantive reasons for the differing conclusions. Many of the studies correlate internal and external conflict for all or most countries in the world, some put nations into different groups for analysis, and others zero in on specific regions or even nations.

— All of the research concerns internal and external conflict *behavior*, not issues or other possible properties of conflict.

— The original Rummel (1963) study employed factor analysis, a method for reducing large arrays of data to a smaller set of basic factors or dimensions. Many of the later studies followed Rummel's basic strategy and also used factor analysis. The nature and limits of this technique should be kept in mind (Stohl 1980).

— The many ways in which internal and external conflict might be related (for example, does external conflict reduce or increase internal conflict?) have not been analyzed systematically and comprehensively.

— Most damaging of all is the frequently offered criticism that this research has not been grounded directly in any kind of a theory. Quantitative event data have been subjected to a number of transformations and statistical techniques. What it all means has been determined in a very *ad hoc* fashion, with the statistical results being presented but without theory guiding the research or interpreting the results.

In addition to the many studies which have probed relationships between external conflict and domestic conflict in general, some have tried to ascertain whether or not *war has a discernible effect on domestic conflict*. At least two alternative explanations are available. One is that war promotes domestic stability and peace through an outgroup/ingroup dynamic in which conflict with an external group promotes cohesion within the group. Stein (1976) identifies a number of factors which affect the war–domestic peace relationship. Overall, there is no direct or clear support for this idea (Stohl 1980). The second explanation is that war promotes conflict within nations and actually maximizes the prospects for extreme collective violence and revolution. Tilly (1978) and many others note the close tie between war and revolution. Stohl (1975) tests this idea in detail by tracing the impact of the United States' involvement in war on domestic political violence in the period from 1890 to 1970. He discovers significant changes in domestic violence at the start of all five major wars during the period and also in the post-war periods, although the exact patterns are not identical. For example, the extent of economic violence went down with the outbreak of both World Wars I and II, but rose in duration at the start of the Korean and Spanish–American Wars.

Stohl's (1975) findings are both statistically significant and substantively interesting. He also anchors the research in a plausible explanation of why war is expected to have an effect on domestic violence: by bringing new groups into the economic production process, increasing the status of underdogs, and producing economic and social changes (which lead to demands for changing the distribution of political power and therefore increase conflict and violence). With World War I, World War II, Korea, and Vietnam, violence between the top and bottom groups in US society increased. But Stohl's research is limited:

— What about other societies? War could be expected to have even greater effects on domestic change and violence in dependent countries, if the prediction of the world system school is valid.
— The approach defines war as a real world version of an experimental stimulus, a causal agent which intrudes occasionally and affects the dependent variable (in this case, domestic conflict and violence). Whether war exerts an effect can be determined with the method used; the actual strength of the association cannot be estimated.

Various *forms of economic and political penetration* have also been considered as determinants of internal violence. Skocpol (1979) and the other qualitative explanatory analysts include international political and economic pressures as a determinant of revolution, with international pressures and internal structural forces (agrarian social structure, state structure and goals, elite structure) interacting to set the stage for a revolutionary situation. Many societal and psychological theorists, however, limit their focus to what goes on within nations in their efforts to explain collective violence. Kerbo (1978) criticizes Olson (1963), Huntington (1968), and others who have emphasized modernization and social change for their implicit adoption of an advanced society model for studying Third World states. They attribute internal stress to the dislocations which come with the early stages of development, an interpretation which does not necessarily fit dependent Third World or periphery nations, which face a completely new and different set of realities.

There are a number of studies of specific forms of external economic and military penetration and their effects on political instability. Military intervention is one form of external involvement which has attracted a great deal of attention. Weede (1978) postulates a causal chain in which general societal weakness leads to domestic disorder and disorder in turn is associated with being a victim of foreign military intervention. In explaining US military intervention in support of the regime between 1958 and 1965, the major determinant is domestic disorder. American aid is very weakly related to intervention, with economic and military assistance apparently being more a reaction to perceived target needs than an instrument for maintaining order in conjunction with intervention. Among the general findings on military intervention and domestic violence are (Stohl 1980):

— conditions within the target country are closely related to external intervention;
— more extreme internal conflict elicits more intervention than 'routine' conflict such as coups; and
— there is general agreement across a number of studies that external intervention increases domestic conflict.

The research on economic dependence suggests clearly that dependence has an indisputable influence on a country's pattern of domestic instability (Kick 1980; Stohl 1980). There is evidence that US private economic penetration promoted anti-US riots, demonstrations, and terrorism in Latin America between the years 1956 and 1965 (Tai *et al.* 1973). Doran's (1978) study of eight Caribbean and Central American nations shows that US military and economic aid is related to the occurrence of guerrilla warfare. Rowe (1974) analyzes coup behavior in eighty-five Third World nations and finds that US military assistance makes coups less likely in military regimes but more likely in civilian regimes. Aside from Gurr, whose work will be discussed shortly as an example of a general model of instability, few studies on dependence attempt to assess the impact of economic penetration in the context of other potential determinants of instability. Russett and his associates on the Yale 'Dependencia' project are trying to map the causes and consequences of dependency.

Thus far, we do know that the extent and especially the forms of instability are related to a nation's role in the international economic system. Advanced or core states differ from those on the periphery, with the expectation that semi-peripheral nations (industrializing Third World states) will show a pattern different from and perhaps between the core and the periphery. Kick (1980) offers a preliminary model which combines the world system and group mobilization approaches. The model assumes that the nation's political and economic characteristics and its role in the world system will shape the accumulation and use of resources and other processes central to the collective action theory of instability. Foreign penetration interacts with the national political economy to affect the scope and form of organized political activity within a country. This model has not been tested, however.

An assessment of the dependence approach is perhaps premature. The existing quantitative research consists mainly of studies of a particular region and form of penetration for spans of a decade or so. However, we can offer a few generalizations:

— How to integrate the dependence approach into existing models and theories is an unanswered question. Kick (1980) offers a useful point of departure, but it is only a beginning.
— The core/semi-periphery/periphery classification reaffirms the importance of searching for explanatory patterns within broad types of nations rather than across all nations at once.
— Analysis across time is especially important for dependence research. As with too much of the quantitative work, existing studies are time-bound and do not trace relationships across time.
— We can juxtapose internal determinants with explanatory factors external to the nation. Both are undoubtedly relevant to explaining political instability. The question is not really

which is more important but how the two interact. Domestic characteristics and processes influence and reflect international factors (Kick 1980: 175). But how does this happen? What are the mechanisms linking the two?
— Transnational economic relations are exerting more and more impact on developed and developing nations. How does this affect the relevance of theories developed prior to the dramatic increases in the extent and intensity of dependence and interdependence?

Most of the quantitative explanatory studies considered up to this point have dealt with one or several sets of internal or external determinants of political instability. *We now shift the focus to 'causal models' of instability.* These are efforts that involve the application of sophisticated analytical techniques to large data sets. Causal modeling allows us to measure the simultaneous impact of many factors that are potential causes of instability. Instead of simple relationships (for example, factor X is associated with instability), we can analyze complex relationships (for example, factors X and Z are associated with political instability, X also affects Z, and X thus impacts on instability directly as well as through Z).

Causal models can become very elaborate and the statistical techniques very advanced. However, it is essential that we remember that constructing a model—the process of identifying the various influences and drawing out their possible relationships—is in a sense much more important than the mechanics of testing the model and getting statistical results. Nowhere is the 'garbage in–garbage out' principle more relevant than in causal modeling. Furthermore, model construction requires extensive expertise about the subject matter as well as insight, creativity, and resourcefulness. Only two instability causal modeling efforts—those of Douglas Hibbs (along with a related effort by David Sanders) will be reviewed here.

Mass Political Violence, which reports the Hibbs (1973) results, moves from partial theories which test aspects of the model to a series of causal models which attempt to explain in a rigorous, comprehensive fashion two dimensions of collective violence: collective protest and internal war. Hibbs uses domestic violence event data for 108 countries for two periods

(1948–57 and 1958–67) and considers a variety of primarily society-level 'causes':

- Levels and rates of change in socio-economic development:
  - economic development;
  - rate of economic change;
  - socio-economic change;
  - urbanization;
  - rate of population growth;
- Social structure imbalances:
  - imbalance in education and economic development;
  - imbalance in urbanization and economic development;
  - social mobilization, government performance, and mass social welfare;
- Socio-cultural diversity:
  - ethnic and language diversity;
  - political separatism;
  - group discrimination;
- The behavior of political elites:
  - coercive capability (for example, military manpower per 10,000);
  - elite repression (censorship, restrictions);
  - coups;
- Political democracy:
  - electoral accountability;
  - mass turnout;
  - democratic political development;
  - communist regime;
  - size of the communist party membership; and the
  - size of the non-communist left.

For each of the five clusters, Hibbs develops and tests simple models of political violence. For the first cluster, he finds a variety of relationships and a few are clear in impact and statistically strong. The rate of population growth does show a fairly strong effect, increasing the amount of both protest and internal war. Social welfare (measured by such indicators as calories per capita and physicians per million) reduces political violence. In general, the pattern for social structure imbalances is weak. In the area of socio-cultural diversity, diversity affects political separatism and separatism increases political violence (especially internal war). No strong causal relationship of any kind emerges for elite coercive capability and political violence. Coups and mass violence are strongly related. Neither electoral accountability nor mass electoral turnout has a significant influence (alone or in combination) on political violence. Democratic political development seems to exert no real effect on protest, but it does reduce internal war. The presence of a communist regime significantly decreases both protest and internal war (especially the latter).

Through a series of increasingly demanding statistical tests, Hibbs also develops a set of core models which excludes those factors which turn out to be statistically insignificant. For example, political violence shows no systematic relationship with the rate of economic growth. High non-defense government expenditures (the indicator for government performance) do not guarantee domestic stability; nor does a high level of social welfare. High protest in the recent past does not explain current protest levels, but past internal war does account for current internal war. In Hibbs' final model, repression, coups, protest, and internal war show a number of noteworthy relationships. Both types of protest evoke elite repression (particularly collective protest). Collective protest leads to repression, which in turn is very strongly associated with internal war.

In addition to the core model results, Hibbs' final conclusions include:

— Past repression has a very strong effect on current internal war, with high repression associated with the lack of internal war.
— The communist regime influence clearly reduces both protest and internal war.
— A high rate of economic growth reduces protest somewhat (but not internal war).
— High elite electoral accountability definitely limits repression.
— Economic development is associated with a decline in the level of violence through the development-democratization-decline in violence causal sequence.
— Past internal war increases present internal war.
— The most important determinant of coups is past coups.

The Hibbs (1973) models are complex and comprehensive; his techniques are rigorous and sophisticated; the research is painstaking and detailed. However, quite a few problems surface in an assessment of the work. Note that the strategy is to analyze over 100 countries at two time points. In a critique of the study, Sanders (1978) raises the question of whether a single generalization can ever characterize all nations and re-analyzes the Hibbs model by breaking the data down into months, which provides 240 cases per country. Instead of a sophisticated causal modeling technique, Sanders simply estimates correlations for each country. He specifies full and partial support and refutation conditions with respect to the Hibbs results and finds that, of 342 cases in his test, only 21 percent meet the full support condition.

Four central criticisms of the Hibbs (1973) study can be identified:

— Sanders (1978) illustrates the dangers of comparing all countries at once.
— Sanders (1978) also demonstrates that very complex models tested at a single point in time can generate highly misleading and even wrong conclusions. By breaking the data down into months rather than years, he is able to look directly at relationships across time. He finds that a number of the patterns do not meet the conditions specified in the Hibbs model.
— What is left out of a model is as important as what goes into it. Hibbs could only include factors that were easily quantifiable and for which data existed across more than 100 countries. As he notes in his conclusion, socio-economic inequality data were therefore excluded. Of special concern is the total neglect of potential external causes of instability.
— On the other hand, the Hibbs model throws in just about everything but the kitchen sink. A good model is complex enough to account for reality but simple enough to be comprehensible.

Sanders (1981), who offers a much more theoretically-grounded analysis than Hibbs', takes essentially the same macro-causal approach. His generally discouraging results illustrate the inescapable limitations of this kind of cross-sectional quantitative research. Generally, Sanders discovers that violent challenge has little effect on peaceful challenge, regime change shows little or no relationship with any other dimension of instability, and the results provide some support for the Hibbs linkage in which the sequence is from peaceful to violent challenge and then to regime change. Also, less severe instability tends to escalate to more intense forms in the Third World, whereas strong and stable political institutions presumably inhibit such escalation in developed societies.

Sanders uses a variety of standard aggregate explanatory variables—including sets of indicators for political and socioeconomic development, dependency, government coercion, and inequality and ethnolinguistic division—in distinct tests of peaceful challenge, violent challenge, government change, and regime change instability. Regional effects are also incorporated. The four models achieve only modest levels of statistical predictability. Interestingly, the highest R^2 is the one for the regime change model, reinforcing other studies where more serious forms of instability are accounted for more adequately than less structured variants.

The work of Ted Robert Gurr (1968a, 1968b, 1970; Gurr and Duvall 1973) on 'relative deprivation' and political instability provides the basis for a causal model which has undergone a considerable amount of testing and refinement. Relative deprivation refers to the perception of a discrepancy between what a person wants and what he or she gets. Just deserts frustration—the failure to achieve what one wants *and* feels entitled to—is advanced as the crucial initial factor. If the person feels that he or she is not getting what is seen as 'just deserts' with respect to important goods and conditions of life, the size of the gap is large, and the person blames the government for this situation, just deserts frustration is at a maximum (Muller 1980). According to Gurr, such frustration produces anger and possibly political aggression—if certain conditions are present. Government forces or coercive potential can limit collective violence if its magnitude is high enough. Institutionalization (such factors as labor union membership and the stability of the party system) increases opportunities for people to get what they want and also provides acceptable routines for expressing discontent. What Gurr calls facilitation refers to factors that promote collective violence (for example, past levels of violence, communist party status, external support for rebels, a country's terrain and transportation network). Finally, regime legitimacy also plays a role, inflating the level of violence if low and reducing it if high. Deprivation is the key determinant of internal violence. It operates through four conditioning factors (coercive potential, institutionalization, facilitation, and legitimacy) and determines violence. The factor to be explained —the magnitude of civil strife—is defined as all collective, non-governmental attacks on persons or property (excluding events involving less than 100 individuals). In his initial work, Gurr breaks strife down into turmoil, conspiracy, and internal war and considers such basic aspects as duration and intensity. He measures deprivation not with attitude data (which are unavailable on a cross-national basis) but with indicators of:

— Persisting deprivation (lack of educational opportunities, religious divisions, economic and political discrimination).
  Short-term economic and political deprivation (trade, inflation, and GNP growth rate indicators, adverse economic conditions, new governmental limits on participation and representation).

The results of the model for 114 countries (including some colonies) in the 1961–5 period are very encouraging, with persisting deprivation alone explaining a lot of the variance in civil strife (Gurr 1968a). In regression analysis, the R^2 statistic, which varies from 0 to 100, measures the 'variance explained.' Persistent deprivation accounts for 24 percent of the total variance, all of the deprivation variables together explain 36 percent, and the addition of legitimacy, the fourth psychological factor, increases the percentage to 43. Overall, the five factors which function as determinants explain 64 percent of the variance in civil strife or collective violence, a quite respectable figure in social science research (at the same time, it is always instructive to point out what amount of the variance is not explained in quantitative-statistical research; in this case, Gurr's model failed to explain 36 percent of the variance).

In more recent tests, the model has been refined considerably (Gurr and Duvall 1973; Gurr and Lichbach 1979). Instead of testing only for one-way causal relationships (for example, deprivation *causes* civil strife), relationships of mutual influence have been included where appropriate. For example, civil conflict and external intervention cause each other and, through intervention, affect social stress (short-term deprivation). Indirect effects are also considered. Economic development, a new factor introduced into the later models, has a positive direct impact on collective violence and a much stronger negative effect (reducing violence) through its causal connections with stress and other factors. For Gurr, the primary determinants of the *extent* of conflict are discontent (deprivation), dispositions toward conflict (beliefs about the desirability and utility of conflict), and the organizational strength of the dissidents. The major factors which explain the *intensity* of conflict are the extent of challenges to the regime, the disposition of elites to react forcefully (whether the regime is a democracy or autocracy), and regime organizational strength. The models developed and tested most recently explain the extent and intensity of protest and rebellion.

The Gurr research has encountered a barrage of criticism, especially from the advocates of collective action theory, who take a group/political process approach, and also from the comparative historical-sociological researchers (discussed earlier in the section on qualitative explanatory research). Eckstein (1980) and Snyder (1978) offer especially detailed and fair critiques. Many of the criticisms are valid, but the more strident attackers fail to demolish the research nearly as effectively as they think. The most frequently raised criticism is that relative deprivation is measured indirectly (with indicators of objective deprivation) rather than directly (with public opinion data). Among the many additional negative comments are the following:

- The research does not follow countries across time, but compares them at a single point in time.
- Although economic development and other characteristics of nations are plugged in, the model does not really take region or type of nation factors into account.
- Many critics point to a number of excluded factors.
- The theory applies to the national level and does not measure conflict between groups within a society at all.
- The process by which frustrations are changed into collective actions is nowhere spelled out (Aya 1979).
- Aya (1979) identifies what he feels are several dubious assumptions in the work, including the idea that a 'revolutionary state of mind' is the fundamental cause of collective violence and the supposition that the potential for mass

revolt is a function of the general level of individual anger and hostilities, which varies with the sum total of individual deprivations in a society.

— The evidence for relative deprivation as a determinant of individual political violence is weak. As we noted earlier, Muller (1980) finds certain beliefs to be crucial; relative deprivation adds very little to the power of those beliefs about the utility of violence to explain aggressive political participation.

— Generally, the theory explains why violence occurs, not how the process operates. This criticism is especially relevant to the context of Aya's (1979) contention that Gurr's and similar approaches neglect the specific balance of political forces within society, the key factor in Tilly's (1978) emphasis on shifting power balances between politically mobilized groups.

— The model is much weaker for explaining protest than rebellion.

— In comparison with Tilly's (1978) theory, Eckstein (1980) concludes that the expectations of both fail to hold consistently or clearly. Neither one 'wins' in a direct contest, although the lack of genuinely valid tests for both plays a role in this conclusion (Snyder 1978).

We can also offer some of the strengths of the Gurr research:

— Unlike much of the instability research (including all of the other psychological theories), the model is derived directly from a theoretical orientation.

— The theory has been carefully developed, tested, and refined over time. Both empirical (model tests) and theoretical standards have been relied on in this process.

— The theory incorporates many of the central factors identified in a number of partial theories and studies which test single hypotheses.

— The concepts are measured carefully and creatively, with multiple rather than single indicators.

— The model includes complex relationships (for example, 'two-way,' testing relationships *among* the detemining factors rather than just treating each as an unrelated cause of political violence).

— The statistical techniques used have been increasingly power-ful and, in a statistical sense, the results have been impressive.

In order to summarize this very large section usefully, it is important to distinguish between explanations of political insta-bility traceable to intranational events and conditions and those traceable to international and global events and conditions. Intranational events and conditions are economic, social, politi-cal, and psychological. Economic event research has concentrated on the explanatory impact of short-term economic change, the level of economic development in a country, economic growth rates, and a country's level of socio-economic inequality. All of this research has merit but a lot of it is also contradictory. Often the 'statistically significant' is completely atheoretical.

Explanations have also been traced to societal problems such as cleavages, structural imbalances, and modernization. Some very noteworthy analysts—like Huntington—believe that modernization leads to political instability, while some less publicized ones have carefully exposed many false and mis-leading assumptions inherent in the modernization school of thought.

Political development analysts have generally focused upon the level of democratization and durability present in a nation, as well as upon how well or badly the political system performs and how legitimate it is perceived to be. The results here have been contradictory and counterintuitive. For example, nations incapable of satisfying basic demands and held in low esteem by their citizens often persist over time.

The 'psychological-aggregate' approach to the study of politi-cal instability has stressed the importance of the frustration-aggression hypothesis of human behavior in the context of national political behavior. When citizens feel 'deprived' they can be expected to become discontented and sometimes collectively violent, but the evidence for this sequence of behavior is thin—largely because of the way the research has been conducted, not necessarily because the basic hypo-theses are wrong.

Research into the effect that elites can have upon political instability has focused upon elite-initiated coups and revolu-tions and, on the other side of the coin, elite repression. The evidence seems to suggest that protest and rebellion lead to elite behavior that can accelerate or undermine the process of political instability.

External determinants of political instability include economic and political penetration, war, and the contagious effects of conflict. While a lot of wars and conflict tend to occur non-randomly throughout history, it would be unwise to overemphasize the 'contagion effect' of intranational and international conflict. The relationship between intranational and international conflict has also been studied extensively with little or no verifiable results.

Finally, causal models of instability have been used to explain intranational conflict with only limited success, largely because they are methodologically and statistically cumbersome.

Quantitative prediction

The quantitative analyst who wishes to forecast political instability has a lengthy menu of objective quantitative forecasting techniques available (Andriole 1983). The techniques range from the simple extrapolative types, which project the present into the future on the basis of assumed current trends, to a series of increasingly advanced and powerful statistical methods. This section will focus upon the following:

— some important analytical distinctions about quantitative prediction and forecasting;
— foreign domestic event data-based computerized systems for forecasting political instability;
— a leading indicators approach to prediction.
— the use of causal models; and the
— use of simulation for predicting domestic instability.

Some philosophers claim that if you can explain something, then in principle you can predict or forecast it. By their very nature, of course, regression and causal models involve the use of an array of independent variables to predict a dependent variable. In practice, however, explanation and prediction are different. Tilly (1975: 485) asserts that this is the case when we try to explain past instances of instability to anticipate future ones:

Whether we are trying to anticipate or to manipulate the political weather, it is quite easy to confuse two different procedures. The first is the explanation of a particular conflict or class of conflicts by moving backward from the effect of the complex of causes which lies behind it: Why the Whiskey Rebellion? Why the recurrent military coups in Latin America? The question is *restrospective*, moving from outcome to origin. The second procedure is the assessment of the probable consequences of a given set of circumstances: What effect does rapid industrialization have on the nature or frequency of protest? What sorts of power struggles tend to follow losses in war? What is this year's likelihood of a rebellion in South Africa, under suppositions *A*, *B*, or *C* about her relations with the rest of the world? These questions have a *prospective* character, moving from origin to outcome—or more likely, to a set of outcomes varying in probability.

Several important realities should be kept in mind. There are many books and articles on forecasting methods, including a number of handbooks devoted to forecasting in general or a particular method. There are also many forecasting exercises in content areas ranging from technology and demography to economics and politics. Less numerous, however, are assessments of the success or failure of particular forecasts. It is amazing how often people write about how to forecast or report actual forecasts—and how rare and after-the-fact evaluations usually are.

The five efforts to forecast political instability presented here use quantitative, 'objective' data (that is, from sources like newspapers, almanacs, United Nations publications, yearbooks of various kinds, and other compendia of statistical information rather than from human experts) and some form of statistics-based analysis. The first involves the use of event data, the second relies on advance warning or leading indicators, the third employs causal modeling, and the fourth and fifth produce forecasts with the technique of simulation. None of the five is completely validated or extensively enough tested to permit us to offer any judgments about the scientific status of the approach; questions of analytical utility will be considered in Part III.

As we pointed out in our brief overview of the *event data approach* for profiling or quantitatively describing political instability, an event is a single episode in which an actor within a country acts in some way toward a target. The action may be verbal or physical and cooperative or conflictual. The event information may be extracted from any source which reports about what goes on in the world.

A project on Africa involved the coding of domestic event data from two prestige newspapers (*New York Times* and *The Guardian*), FBIS (Foreign Broadcast Information Service) *Daily Reports*, and cable traffic (Hopple 1980a). (Some data were also taken from Reuters and several African event chronologies; only the open source data will be discussed here.) The event data approach is a good way of describing or monitoring the current status of a nation's domestic politics. Events sent to and received from the government, military, media, mass public, and other key groups can be counted and displayed. Trends in conflict, cooperation, and such important indicators as tension (the percentage of all events which are conflictual) can be surveyed and mapped. Overall patterns for the country as a whole and for specific sub-national actors and targets can be easily delineated. For forecasting purposes, the event data set is used as a source of objective information for extrapolating trends into the short-range future. The driving assumption in such an event-based 'early warning system' is that the immediate future will be like the recent past. If conflict begins, it is assumed that it will go on. In addition, certain indicators in the system may function as 'leading indicators.' If tension goes up or if conflict rises a lot compared to its normal level, this may provide 'early warning' of impending conflict. Unfortunately, the African system was never really evaluated as a forecasting tool. Past research on Japan and Peru indicated that the event approach has some utility from the perspective of accurate short-term forecasting.[15] However, the approach is so simple, conceptual difficulties so pervasive, and the actual results so mixed, given the time and resources required, that a rational cost–benefit evaluation would probably argue against such an approach. Among the many problems with event data forecasting of political instability from the vantage point of purely 'scientific' assessment criteria are the following:

— What are we trying to forecast? Actual events or general trends? Deviations from normality? Internal crises?
— How do you evaluate the performance of such a system? How do you determine what reality is—even after the fact?
— How damaging is the simplified extrapolation mechanism that is built into the system's forecasting capability?

— What is the best way to deal with 'false alarms' and 'misses'?
— How well can a system perform if it consists exclusively of events (records of what happened) and excludes situations and conditions which lead to and cause the events?
— All forecasting methods have real problems with the unexpected, the discontinuous, and the unprecedented. This is especially true when you deal with rare events like internal crises and revolution. Probably the *worst* kind of a system for handling these types of problems is one which leaves out *causal* factors and relies on simple extrapolation.

Abolfathi *et al.* (1980) provide an example of an approach based upon leading or anticipatory indicators as the source of early warning signals about potential instability. Specifically, they consider three types of leading indicators—stock markets, the weighted average of interest rates on loans to Third World countries (or the 'spread' over the London Interbank Offer Rate or LIBOR), and international credit ratings of borrowing countries. Given the immediate concerns of investors and international bankers and the self-interest involved (as well as the presumed frequent access to special and well-placed sources of information), these kinds of indicators can be expected to be both timely and relevant. They may serve as valid indicators of a country's 'danger' of experiencing severe political stress and upheaval. Abolfathi *et al.* also look in detail at two particular countries, Egypt and the Philippines. In addition to leading indicators of instability, they are also interested in indicators of:

— The government's capacity to govern:
    — efficiency and government legitimacy;
    — adequacy of governmental revenues;
— Indicators of political environment:
    — government reports of plots and conspiracies against it;
    — issue positions of major political groups in the country;
    — public opinion data;
— Indicators of the social environment (when available):
    — crime rate, and so forth;
— Indicators of the economic environment:
    — inflation;
    — balance of payments;
    — debt service burden;

— urban unemployment; and
— budget deficits.

How does this indicators approach fare? Abolfathi *et al.*
report the success or failure of the various leading and other
indicators in the two countries between 1945 and 1980. They
judge the indicators not only in terms of their historical and
current performance but also with respect to the criteria of how
reasonable, useful, and available they are. For the Philippines,
they evaluate the indicators' performance prior to and during
four periods of high instability (the Huk rebellion during the
late 1940s and 1950s, the student turmoil of the late 1960s, the
increasing lawlessness and insurgency during the early 1970s,
and periods of high insurgency since). The test for Egypt
includes four distinct manifestations of instability (the turmoil
from 1949 to 1952 which led to the revolution, several periods
of Moslem extremist activism, three phases of general regime
weakness, periods of major riots and lawlessness). Both stock
market activities and international credit ratings work pretty
well for Egypt and the Philippines. Stock market indicators
correctly foresaw the upsurge of instability in the early 1970s
in the Philippines (as did private construction activities). In
Egypt, stock market patterns generally predicted several periods
of political instability and government policy change. Trends
through the end of the 1970s suggested increasing instability
in the Philippines and pervasive uncertainty about Egypt.

There are also leading indicators which really do 'lead'
(point to impending instability before it hits) and good indicators of government capacity and political, social, and economic
trends which monitor very effectively (and sometimes lead).
The results of the project by Abolfathi and his colleagues,
which they refer to as a feasibility study, are quite encouraging.
However, we must offer a few cautions:

— Case studies are good for certain things and not so good for
  others. They are good for taking a detailed look at a particular situation (especially if there has been a lot of preceding
  basic research). They are bad for generalizing or explaining
  systematically (unless used explicitly in a comparative historical sense, which was not the approach here).[16]
— With a pure indicator approach, we can tell what works or
  doesn't work (whether an indicator anticipates or tracks).

We cannot ascertain exactly what influences what or identify the causal patterns. Some argue that the latter is trivial or unnecessary. However, the ability to determine more complex causal relationships not only allows us to have more confidence in the results—it also guards against premature reliance on a misleading indicator reading.[17]

We have already introduced and discussed in some detail Ted Robert Gurr's model of instability. Gurr and Lichbach (1979) use this basic *causal model for forecasting* the extent and intensity of protest and rebellion in the 1971–5 period. They select a sample of ten countries from the larger group of eighty-six and measure the causal factors for the year 1970. They then estimate the predicted levels of conflict for the ten nations and compare the forecasted conflict with the actual internal conflict for the 1971–5 span. Employing two statistical tests to determine the actual amount of forecasting error, Gurr and Lichbach conclude that, in general, the forecasting errors are no worse than the ones for all eighty-six nations in the basic test period (1961–5, with the causal factors measured primarily around 1960). Rebellion is forecast better than protest, intensity better than extent, and cases close to the average better than extreme cases. While the model performs adequately as a forecasting tool, quite a few specific countries are not predicted well at all. For the extent of protest, Argentina and Italy were very high during both eras in reality, but the model underestimated both cases. For 1971–5, the extent of rebellion was too high for Kenya and Egypt, with far less rebellion occurring than predicted. In contrast, the model failed to forecast accurately the extent of rebellion for Pakistan and Argentina in the other direction—with more actually occurring than predicted. For Brazil, the forecast and actual results corresponded pretty closely, with little significant potential for extensive rebellion present in either the model or the real world. Yugoslavia, another country often thought to be a prime candidate for instability, shows low forecast and actual rebellion in both 1961–5 and 1971–5.

The use of causal modeling to forecast political instability is in its infancy. This example illustrates both successes and failures. Factors are almost always left out of models, factors which will usually affect some countries more than others.

Furthermore, a model predicts what it explains best. Not surprisingly, the forecasts for the rebellions, which are better explained, are much more accurate than those for protest. By its very nature, a causal model-generated forecast is more accurate for countries close to the average. This is an inherent and very unfortunate limitation of the methodology—political instability analysis is concerned to a great extent with nations far away from the 'average.'

Forecasts produced by statistical models have a number of intrinsic weaknesses and strengths, as the Gurr–Lichbach exercise demonstrates. Three points are worth noting:

— Such models are very useful for placing countries on scales or injecting a comparative perspective. How unstable is Yugoslavia compared to Kenya? Why is instability predicted accurately for Brazil but not for Egypt? If Pakistan is predicted to have instability at one point but doesn't have it (as was the case for 1961-5), it may have it later (as Pakistan did, with the civil war and secession of Bangladesh during the later period). (But we rarely if ever seem to be able to isolate these kinds of anomalies ahead of time—that is, sort out the cases where the 'forecast' does not come true now but does later from the instances where the forecast comes to pass neither now nor later.)

— You need data to forecast. You not only need a good bit of data, but you must have at least some data for the present. To forecast instability in 1982, you need data at the least for causal factors in 1980 or 1981.

— Also, causal model forecasting is expensive and time consuming. The proper integration and use of such forecasts requires at the least some knowledge of econometrics. Cost–benefit considerations and tradeoffs are usually highly relevant and never totally irrelevant. Can you afford it? Is it worth it even if you can?

Dahlgren's (1976, 1978) work should be mentioned briefly at this point. Gurr and Lichbach (1979) use statistical data to forecast conflict. Dahlgren conducted a pilot study which relied on expert assessments to test an earlier but basically similar version of the Gurr model as a potential 'intelligence aid in the analysis of political violence' (Dahlgren 1976: 1). Dahlgren used intelligence specialists as data sources. Analysts assisted in providing subjective inputs to the model, which included Gurr's central concepts of relative deprivation, beliefs about the justifiability of violence, the amount of coercive force available, and institutional support available. Judgments were elicited for each group thought to be of importance in the particular country. The average scores of the analysts became the 'input' and thus served as indicators for the determinants, capabilities, and potential for political violence, the elements of Gurr's model. The model was applied to Chile in mid-1973 and to Argentina, Ethiopia, and Thailand at monthly intervals from November 1974 to June 1975. Although the model apparently did pick up gross trends in the countries studied, the 'data' (the expert assessments) were marked by a lot of disagreement between and among the experts. The extensive overall lack of agreement held up across countries, time periods, and types of internal groups. Nor did the model's predictions show impressive relationships with actual behavior patterns in the nations studied.

Rastogi (1977) presents an interesting model of instability. His model *uses simulation to generate forecasts of future trends.*[18] Rastogi's concern is with political stability and the more basic issue of the viability of societies. His model features a number of core factors related directly and indirectly to the dynamics of societies and governmental change and instability patterns. Among the factors are public expectations, administrative effectiveness, pressure on the government from several sources, economic trends such as inflation, unemployment, and general growth, population growth, and several additional forces. Rastogi delineates past, present, and future time paths (1960–80) for four nations—Brazil, India, Nigeria, and the United States—to illustrate how his simulation model operates. He is able to explain patterns retrospectively through 1975 and then offers sets of possible courses for the four societies from 1976 to 1980. For Brazil, which we regard here as the example, Rastogi outlines a future course which assumes the simple continuation of current trends. The pattern projects a continuing decline in what he calls politico-military pressure, an increase in economic growth and the investment of external capital, and a continuing high rate of population growth. Problems of inflation and public unrest will not be resolved. Under these conditions, random external and internal forces may increase the pressure on the system, with Brazil possibly returning to the chaotic pattern which prevailed during the early 1960s.

An alternative course for Brazilian society is also sketched out. This path involves an increase in pressure. Inflation continues to go up, as does unemployment. Public unrest and ethnic tension rise, accompanied by declines in economic growth, stability of the government, and public expectations. External investments are assumed to stop after the second year into the future. From the second year on, serious political instability and many governmental changes are predicted.

Allan and Stahel (1983) present a second example of simulation-based instability forecasting. Whereas Rastogi is concerned with general societal instability, Allan and Stahel deal with the problem of forecasting guerrilla war outcomes. Using Afghanistan as an example, they account for and project two behaviors: macrocombat interactions between the Afghan guerrillas and the Soviet and Afghan armies and the level of support for the guerrillas.

The model which they develop is a simple dynamic mathematical model which is a priori and deductive rather than statistical-empirical (although the fit between their estimates and reality from 1980–2 is very high). The model is grounded in empirical information from other similar events (the guerrilla war experiences of South Sudan, Malaysia, Vietnam, and Yugoslavia). The overall 1980–2 model simulation yields scenarios which generally show that the guerrillas are fairly successful across the entire time period and inflict relatively heavy losses on Soviet forces. Only a very large Soviet escalation (over 300,000 troops) could make a real difference, they discover; even then, it would be extremely difficult to crush the resistance because of the depth of support for the guerrillas and the primitive nature of the nation and its economy.

Allan and Stahel attempt to demonstrate the value of their approach for analyzing and forecasting guerrilla warfare. Such an a priori quantitive approach, they maintain, can be employed to rank-order alternative influences, discriminate among competing assumptions by deriving and comparing explicit predictions, and provide a rigorous description of the unfolding dynamics of tribal guerrilla warfare against a colonial power. The evolutionary description or forecast depends on the assumptions, of course, but the latter are at least explicit

—a strength over many qualitative approaches—and can be varied systematically (as can the parameters of the model) to conduct sensitivity tests, explore a variety of 'what-if' questions, and construct various scenarios.

To a great extent, simulation models have not been verified as tools for forecasting political instability. Our balance sheet is therefore premature, but the following pluses and minuses are provisionally set forth:

- The simulation approach facilitates dynamic and complex analysis, enabling the analyst to take both time and causal patterns into account.
- Comparisons can easily be made about different patterns for the same time path (for example, a simple assumption that the status quo will persist versus assuming changes in various factors).
- The second bullet shades into a third advantage: by 'varying the parameters,' as they say, simulation provides a useful and powerful means for constructing all kinds of scenarios. Building plausible scenarios is as important as (some would say more important than) generating trend or point forecasts.
- Inferences can be made about the critical levers in a society. For example, Rastogi finds that most of the problem-associated factors in his Brazil model are not in a state of 'high' or 'hyper' instability, but population growth rate definitely is. Rapid demographic change is therefore the primary cause of Brazil's continuing problem with inflation. Price stability would require a reduction in the rate of population growth from 3.5 percent annually (and, to completely solve the problem, an increase in economic growth to 10 percent a year).
- Simulation models are useful for avoiding the dangers and fallacies of a 'single case fixation' and encourage comparisons —tracking a society across time or contrasting countries.
- *As with all modeling, what goes in determines what comes out.* Assumptions and data quality are both absolutely crucial.
- As with causal modeling, it is necessary to have at least some of the data for the predictive period or just before it, especially in the case of complex models where everything is related to everything else.

— And again, model complexity and cost factors enter in. Is it worth it in terms of cost and pay-off?

Cost-benefit calculations are very difficult to make when it comes to political instability forecasting. Books on forecasting methods offer us tempting matrices for selecting forecasting techniques on the basis of the type of problem and such criteria as time, cost, and data. Simply identify the forecasting goal (short, medium, and long-range), the problem at hand, and assess the relevant criteria—and the matrix leads you magically and effortlessly to a particular method. The problem with political instability is that there have been so few genuine forecasts—and so little evaluation of forecasts—that we lack some of the most basic preliminary information.

The most basic question, of course, is, 'What do you want to forecast?,' which takes us full circle, back to the question of what political instability is—and therefore back to the analytical tasks of description and classification. That, unfortunately, is only the first of many questions—and problems —for the political instability forecaster which will be addressed in the next chapter of the book.

In summary, it is important to acknowledge that prediction is not necessarily a natural outgrowth of successful explanation, as some philosophers of social science maintain. Explanation is by definition a retrospective undertaking while prediction is a prospective one. The methods and techniques appropriate to retrospection and prediction are not inherently compatible.

Event data, for example, are very good descriptors of political instability but generally poor predictors. Quantitative indicators are also better descriptors than predictors. While some case studies have been completed, much remains to be done before any predictive guidelines can be developed. Gurr's causal model of instability is also only minimally successful and in need of a great deal of tuning before we can expect it to yield any reliable predictions. Similarly, Rastogi's simulation and the guerrilla model are experimental.

Part III
An assessment of political instability research methodologies

4 The assessment criteria and blueprint

Godson and Shultz (1981–82) and Godson (1980) identify the four 'classic' elements of government intelligence:

— Clandestine collection—Obtaining valued information from open and denied areas through the use of both human and technological methods.
— Counter-intelligence (CI)—The identification, neutralization, and manipulation of other states' intelligence services. (There is a broader definition, involving the use of CI for positive collection on adversaries' intentions.)
— Analysis and estimates—This process assesses all available data and delivers to policy-makers a finished product that has more clarity than may be inherent in the data itself.
— Covert action (CA)—An attempt to influence politics and events in other states without revealing involvement.

This book is concerned almost exclusively with how the analytical methodologies, approaches, and findings discussed in Part II can be productively applied to the *analysis* of information about political instability and the generation of political instability intelligence *estimates*. This utility assessment will be conducted with the aid of the matrix presented in Figure 4.1. Note how the methodological types discussed in Part II are used in conjunction with two general evaluative criteria: accuracy/verifiability and implementation requirements.

But before we begin it is important to understand what this book will not do. No attempt will be made to deal with the bureaucratic or organizational milieux in and around which intelligence analyses and estimates are produced. This caveat is important because it is widely known that even the best analyses and estimates must pass through a set of bureaucratic/ organizational filters before they can play meaningful roles in the aggregation and production of finished intelligence. We

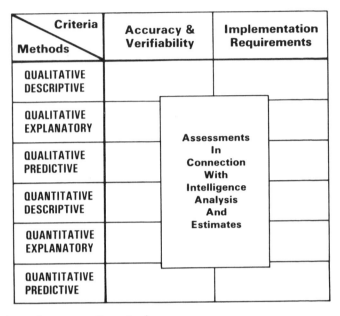

Fig. 4.1   Assessment Organization

will not attempt to identify either the obstacles to or accelerators for intelligence integration and production. Colby, Pipes, Codevilla (all in Godson 1980), and Halperin and Kanter (1973), among others, deal with such issues in ways which far exceed our capabilities.

Finally, the following assessment will concentrate upon known political instability research findings and the methods, approaches, and techniques which facilitate their production. The distinction is important because sometimes apparently significant findings are generated via the misapplication of methods, just as perfectly applied methods can yield insignificant findings. Our assessment will recognize both situations and attempt to suggest how findings can be extended by improved methodological implementation and vice versa.

Accuracy and verifiability

What do we mean by accuracy and verifiability? In the context of descriptive political instability research accuracy should be understood as the degree to which descriptions of political instability or related events and conditions are representative of the phenomena under investigation. The accuracy of explanatory political instability research should be anchored in the degree and consistency of the association between intranational and international events and conditions and various manifestations of political instability. Predictive accuracy is a little easier to determine in so far as events and conditions occur or do not occur. Retrospective predictions are also relatively easy to adjudge accurate or inaccurate.

But there are some problems. First, all accuracy assessments are *context dependent*. Assessments can only be made fairly when the analyst's goals are clearly stated and/or understood. For example, it is not unusual for political instability theorists to pursue *normative* analytical goals. While the pursuit of such goals can be interesting, it is useful to intelligence analysts only when it sheds direct *objective* light upon a defineable intelligence problem. Another assessment issue is related to when a finding was produced and interpreted. Even though our survey and assessment only covers twenty years of political instability research, methods, techniques, and analytical perspectives have changed considerably since 1960. Consequently, the dates when the research was conducted during the following assessment should be noted. No doubt it will be discovered, what the research revealed to us—that there are dramatic, though not necessarily progressive, differences in the research conducted in 1960 from that conducted in the early 1980s.

Interestingly, these concerns apply to both qualitative and quantitative research. Analysts have used both research methodologies to generate normative and objective findings. They have also changed the way they use the methods since 1960.

All of this is inextricably tied to verifiability. But how can research findings be verified? One way involves reproducing the analysis and coming up with the initial results. But when the primary analytical goal is normative, it is impossible to reproduce the results unless the quantitative perspectives of the analysts are identical. But even when the analytical goals are objective it may be impossible to verify the results by reproducing them because there are so many methodological nuances connected with most analyses that unless they are perfectly replicated the results can not be verified; and as has already probably been concluded, perfect replications can be very time-consuming and expensive.

The implications of these accuracy/verifiability problems for our political instability findings/methods assessment include the following:

— The accuracy of specific political instability research findings and general methodologies is relevant to intelligence analysis and estimating to the extent that they can be verified, but verification is impossible in normative situations and difficult in objective ones.

— In order to assess how useful the various findings and methods can be to political instability intelligence analysts, it is necessary to understand the analytical context in which the research was originally conducted.

— Ultimately, verifiability is traceable to the larger literature, where highly related research can be used to determine the utility of a general line of inquiry, and to the experience of the analyst who can often quickly distill research down to its most diagnostic properties.

— Unfortunately, since most of the research presented in our survey has not been verified, it is up to assessments like the following to determine just how useful it can be. But candidly, our assessment necessarily contains some biases; intelligence analysts must thus become involved directly in the assessment process in order to help minimize analytical biases and maximize opportunities for qualitative and quantitative methodological influence in the intelligence analysis and estimates process.

— Any utility assessment of qualitative and quantitative descriptive, explanatory, and predictive political instability research must be very carefully interpreted not just because of the inevitable biases of the assessors but because all utility assessments are at least to some extent judgmental.

Implementation requirements

Our assessment will also address the implementation problem because decisions regarding 'what to believe' and 'how to analyze' should be made in conjunction with assessments about implementation costs. The components of the requirements which determine costs include the following:

— expertise requirements;
— time requirements;
— data requirements; and
— support requirements.

According to Andriole (1983), the important questions about expertise include:

— who?
— what? and
— how good?

Questions regarding 'who?' generally apply first to one's self. In other words, an analyst should be completely aware of his or her own strengths and weaknesses. If one is thoroughly skilled and experienced with the application of several methods and techniques then one should acknowledge that perhaps the strongest talent can be found seated behind one's own desk. On the other hand, if one's skills and experience are limited, then efforts must be made to identify and use talented in-house and outside associates. Ideally, one's internal environment will satisfy most or all expertise requirements; however, such is not always the case. Perhaps too often outside associates are necessary, presenting yet another set of problems. Far too frequently outside associates (consultants and the like) may appear ready, willing, and able to perform specific tasks. Unfortunately, while some experts have mastered a great many analytical techniques, there are just as many who have only a superficial knowledge of and limited experience with systematic analytical methodologies. Every effort must thus be made to identify and select only those outside associates which can meaningfully contribute to the solving of an analytical problem.

It is important to identify specifically those areas of specialization with which the analyst is familiar. Just as importantly, assessments must be made regarding the specific strengths and weaknesses of credible outside associates. The six categories in this report might well be useful for such identification and assessment, recognizing that some individuals are good qualitative describers but relatively poor quantitative predictors. Similarly, it may be that in-house personnel excels at the tasks connected with instability hypothesis formation but is relatively weak in the application of computers to the analysis of political instability.

An extremely difficult question concerns assessments regarding the overall quality of certain individuals. 'How good' someone is depends to a large extent upon his or her *training, skill, real problem-solving experience, and attitude*. While formal academic training is often very useful in the production of analyses and estimates, it does not unto itself qualify an individual as talented: there are many holders of advanced degrees who have long since stopped reading and studying.

One's skills in the application of specific methods and techniques may be a better indicator of how useful one might be as a member of an analytical team. Skillful analysts may or may not have formal training but they frequently have a good deal of real problem-solving experience, the next important criterion. Unlike some academically trained individuals, those who have applied analytical experience tend to be less preoccupied with the development of theory or the pursuit of truth for its own sake; on the contrary, they tend to be excited about the prospect of actually solving a specific analytical problem.

Regardless of how well trained, skillful, or experienced an analyst may be, if his or her attitude is disruptive, overly independent, and/or condescending, among other failings, then he or she is probably not likely to be effective. In fact, it is difficult to underestimate the importance of this criterion. Too frequently individuals with extensive formal training and long résumés are selected to participate in the analytical process with little or no regard for the personality described in his or her supporting materials. One analyst with the wrong attitude can easily inhibit, misdirect, misinform, and otherwise undermine the entire analytical process.

There is no question that the availability and use of *time* is of critical importance to any analytical process. At the most specific level, analysts should be cognizant of the amount of time available and necessary to solve a particular problem. The key is to associate available time with the amount of time required to implement an instability research method or technique. Obviously some methods take longer to implement than others; the amount of available time can and should determine the selection and rejection of alternative methodologies.

All analysis must also be informed by reliable and accessible *data and information*. Data comes in many forms but nearly all of it can be categorized according to its epistemological origins. There is hard, or empirical, data, and soft, or 'expert,' data. We are all familiar with soft data. In its unstructured form, soft data is the essence of experience. Organized according to a set of specific criteria, soft data can take the form of quantitative judgments or opinions. Hard data, on the other hand, is generally derived from the objective observation of selected phenomena in a way which assures reproducibility, verifiability, and validation. An example of each kind might concern the level of rainfall during a particular storm: soft data might result from a polling of meteorologists while hard data might be generated via a rain gauge. A popular misconception regarding soft data is that it cannot or should not be quantitative or manipulated scientifically. In truth, soft data may be as quantitative as hard data and just as susceptible to scientific analysis.

Another misconception concerns the viability of soft versus hard data. In practice, soft data banks, comprised of, for example, judgments about the likelihood of nuclear war during the next ten years, are often at least as useful as more empirical projections. It is thus very difficult to assess the value of hard and soft data. Instead, one should only attempt to do so within the context of particular analytical requirements. For example, when hard data is unavailable, unreliable, or too expensive, available soft data, if relevant, reliable, and affordable, can frequently be used to solve complicated problems. There are also occasions when soft data should be preferred to hard data and vice versa. As a general rule, when a problem is distinguishable by its judgmental characteristics or when virtually no hard precedent data exist, soft data should be preferred. But when a problem is by definition empirical and a great deal of precedent data exists, hard data should be preferred. An example of the first type of problem is a hostage negotiation, while grain forecasting is an example of the second.

Another important consideration regarding the use of (hard and soft) data is its location. For example, frequently a problem may be solved via a less desirable data set primarily because it is available in-house. If time is of the essence, it may be impractical to either acquire or generate data from the outside.

Still another consideration is the *reliability* of the data or information which is to be used to solve a particular problem. Unreliable data, it is believed, can only yield unreliable solutions. This view is false. 'Unreliable' data can in fact yield useful results if the aspects of the unreliability are known prior to its use, and 'reliable' data in the wrong hands can produce disastrous results. At the same time, it is important to remember that all data is to some extent unreliable. Data utility is a function not of precise measures of reliability but rather familiarity; when a problem-solver is very familiar with a particular data set or data base it is likely to be used productively, but when a data set is unfamiliar to a problem-solver it is much more likely to be misused. The same holds true in intelligence analysis. When a particularly good source of information is discovered it is generally relied upon again and again.

We will try to identify the data requirements connected with the use of the methods and techniques of political instability analysis presented in Part II of this book.

Talented analysts with access to necessary data and in full command of methods, approaches, and time, will usually fail unless adequate *support* exists. The overall importance of support is analogous to the computer science notion of through-put, or the processes by which information, decisions, and solutions are formulated and flow through their organizational surroundings. The most important component of support is people. Here the reference is to typing and production support, research support, and administrative or procedural support. Fast, accurate, and reliable people are absolutely necessary for successful analysis.

Information is another kind of support. Ideally, necessary problem-solving information may be acquired in-house; if not, effective means for the creation or acquisition of outside data must be established. If internal procedures are unsupportive or non-supportive, then analysts will find themselves inhibited by unyielding administrative realities. Serious problem-solvers ought not to lose sight of the potential impact of administrative and bureaucratic policies and procedures upon the analysis and estimates process.

Yet another component of support is the number, nature, and quality of available machines. On the mundane side, perhaps, are the typewriters and reproductive machines available for problem-solving use; and on the more sophisticated side, are computerized word processors and other computerized routines useful for effective data storage, manipulation, and analysis. If a secretary has to travel several floors to copy a piece of paper, or retype a page five times without the aid of a memory typewriter, then it is safe to say that the problem-solving process will probably not be consistently competitive.

Some methods require a good deal more support than others. Throughout the following assessment we will identify the routine and special requirements connected with the use of alternative methods and techniques, as suggested generally in Figure 4.2.

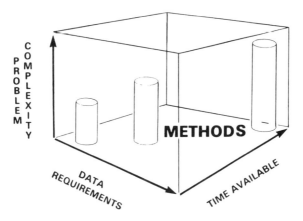

Fig. 4.2   Criteria for Methods Assessment

Assessment blueprint

What follows is organized around the six major research/methods categories used to organize our survey and two general evaluative criteria. Six major sections thus appear below. Within each section the general and specific elements of the evaluative criteria are used to assess how useful the six sets of findings and methods can be to the production of political instability intelligence analyses and estimates. Following this assessment, a set of summary assessments will be developed. These assessments will constitute a completely distilled set of judgments about the findings and methods most likely to contribute to the analysis of political instability. We will also develop rationale for our judgments in this final section.

5 Qualitative description findings/methods assessment

It should be recalled that qualitative research is grounded in the wisdom, judgment, and intuition of the analyst. It is accurate because of this characteristic and unverifiable for the same reason. But it is potentially useful to intelligence analysts.

Accuracy and verifiability

As Goldstone (1980) points out, many of the qualitative case studies that have been produced over the past twenty years or so have yielded incredibly minute details about a 'single case' of political instability. How useful are single case studies?

When carefully conducted, case studies can be very useful, especially when they cover a long period of time. In the social sciences, single case studies are often used to identify hypotheses to be subsequently tested for the purpose of discovering patterns of behavior. If discovered, such patterns can contribute to understanding about what political instability is and how it can be classified. But case studies can satisfy a lot of other analytical requirements as well, especially when there is some doubt about the discovery of trends and some real ambivalence about the need for such discoveries. For example, sometimes rapidly changing political conditions *can only be understood in the context of a larger political history*. The social scientific pursuit of trends and patterns, which is almost always methodologically grounded in aggregate analysis, will 'miss' the significance of individual changes, a significance which case studies can capture.

The whole case study versus aggregate analysis comparison is important to understanding how very different analytical methods and approaches can contribute to intelligence analysis. If one's analytical goals are to acquire detailed descriptions of political instability then case studies should be preferred to aggregate or other broadbrush analysis. But if the analytical problem requires one to identify some general patterns or trends that might have relevance to a particular case then aggregate analyses may be preferred.

But how accurate are case studies? The answer depends upon at least three interrelated factors. First, and contrary to many social and behavioral science notions about methodology, good case study analysis is systematic and precise. It almost always adheres to the historical approach which uses chronology as an ordering device, and more often than not extends beyond the compilation of simple facts and attempts to develop some level of generalization based upon a qualitative analysis of the compiled sequential record. These (high or low-level) generalizations are what are sometimes referred to by laymen as 'lessons from history'. The credibility of the generalizations is traceable to the logic displayed during the process of information gathering and generalization deduction. Beyond logic assessments, consumers of case study analyses should use their own expertise and experience to determine how well or badly the case is constructed.

Case study accuracy assessments must also be made in conjunction with assessments about the purposes of the case study analyst. Some analysts intend to describe events and conditions while others will attempt to generalize well beyond their own case. Fairness demands that we only judge the accuracy of what the analyst intended to produce, not what we might have wished he or she produced. One should also be careful to separate strictly normative purposes and 'findings' from more objective ones.

Finally, accuracy should be determined by an assessment of related case study analyses (if such analyses exist). Such comparisons are analogous to the comparison of replicated analyses though nowhere near as precise.

Some qualitative case studies have yielded definitions of political instability. Tilly's (1975, 1978) work is a case in point. His work on *collective action* provides an excellent basis upon which to build competing definitions. But more important are the *components* of his—and all—definitions which can be used by analysts for reference purposes. For example, Tilly sees collective action, or CA, as comprised of the interests of actors, organization, mobilization, opportunity, and (collective) action. Is this definition of collective action, which is used by Tilly to define political instability, applicable to real world analysis? Probably *the answer depends upon the societal and political system under investigation*. Is the definition accurate? Only if it applies to the problem at hand. *In other words, all definitions of political instability are analytically useful only after they have been passed through a situational filter.* For example, definitions of political instability would be very different for open versus closed and agrarian versus industrialized countries.

All of this also applies to qualitative classifications of political instability. Tilly (1975, 1978) provides an example of a classificatory schema which can be assessed. But as we have already discussed in Part II, his classification does not include spontaneous violence as a classificatory type (see p. 15). Given the evidence that suggests rather convincingly that not all political violence is organized, Tilly's schema is of little applied value unless modified to include both organized *and* spontaneous violence. In terms of accuracy, it is interesting that so much evidence contradicts Tilly's schema, evidence which is as available to Tilly as it is to us. The lesson requires us to once again look to the motives of the analyst. Tilly was trying to develop a theory of political activity based upon theoretical notions of collective action. Applied analysis requires very different priorities.

The usefulness of definitions and classifications also depends upon how well constructed their building blocks—or *concepts* —are. We have already pointed out that Tilly fails to include a large subset of political violence in his definition. Experience and other evidence thus suggest that his concepts are deficient from an applied perspective.

Classifications of revolutions are also only as useful as the criteria used to develop them. Chalmers Johnson's (1964) six kinds of revolution (based upon four criteria: targets, perpetrators, goals, and initiation) are only useful if you accept his classificatory criteria. If not, then perhaps the criteria-based approach to classification may be suggestive of additional criteria or alternative approaches. In fact, several other analysts have already challenged Johnson.

Perhaps the most useful qualitative descriptive research

conducted by the so-called natural history school involves the development of stages of revolutionary activity. Schwartz's (1972) ten stages are illustrative of the results of such research. But why is such research useful? Is it accurate? Can it be verified? *It is useful because it can be used by intelligence analysts to convert definitions and classifications of political instability into active monitoring tools.* While Schwartz's stages constitute a good starting point, the utility lies not in his precise list but in the notion that revolution and political stability can be broken down into analyzable parts. The precise accuracy of previous lists of stages is thus relatively unimportant; much more critical is the verifiability of one's own stages via their use over time as a monitoring device.

A related example of a stage or 'check-off' monitoring system belongs to Belden (1977). As suggested in Figure 5.1, he associates the probability of war with a series of decisions that led up to the Japanese decision to attack Pearl Harbor. While Belden does not attempt to develop a set of 'attack stages', the example suggests that the probability of revolution could be monitored as a society or political system passed through a series of sequential stages.

Implementation requirements

Qualitative analyses are not as easy to conduct as many behavioralists would have us believe. While it is true that expertise in inferential statistics is not often required in qualitative analysis, low-level descriptive statistical expertise frequently is. Relatedly, expertise in the collection and presentation of empirical data is also often required, as is knowledge about how to relate data to insight and generalization. Experience with the use of the historical approach is also required if an analyst's generalizations are to be persuasive and credible.

Qualitative descriptive analyses can also take a lot of time to conduct. If your analytical requirements are short-order then unless a qualitative analysis is in process you will probably only get subjective impressions from an analyst who would assuredly prefer to present the results of a more thorough descriptive analysis. The myth of qualitative analysis is that it is not as methodologically demanding, time-consuming, or, therefore, expensive as quantitative analysis. In practice, qualitative research can be as complicated as quantitative research, although

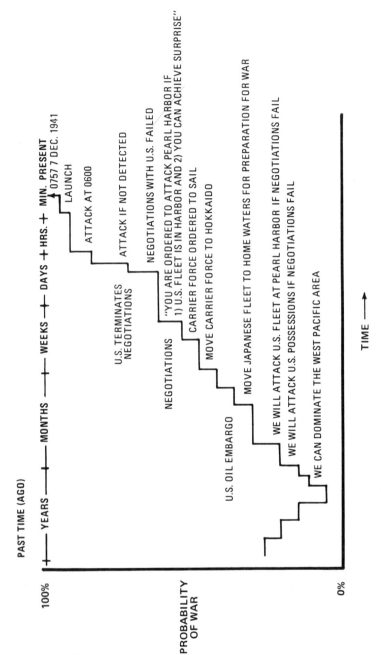

Fig. 5.1 Belden's Decision Stairway

computer-based support requirements are usually much lower for qualitative analysis.

Also, given the academic and professional training that the majority of analysts receive today, one is much more likely to find qualitative analysts than quantitative ones. But one should be alert to the qualitative analyst who believes that good analysis simply involves reading and thinking. Like the quantittive analyst who is predisposed to the use of sophisticated statistical techniques, such an analyst will produce generalizations unlikely to be grounded in systematic observation and insight.

6 Qualitative explanation findings/methods assessment

The qualitative analysts who have tried to explain political instability have focused upon a variety of intranational factors including elite behavior, social class divisions, and terrorist activity. The dominant qualitative method has involved the use of comparative case studies (where there are many variables and a few cases). The results have been mixed.

Accuracy and verifiability

How does one assess the accuracy of Marxist explanations of instability without adopting a set of ideological evaluative criteria? For that matter, how does one assess any explanation grounded in judgments about the moral quality of a political system? Should one even try? We would argue that the values inherent in many of the most widely-known qualitative explanations of political instability are only important to understanding the perspective of the analyst, not necessarily the accuracy of his or her explanations. For example, while Marxist and other 'political philosophies' continue to fuel political rhetoric and action around the world, they also contain ideas that may be relevant to explaining political instability, especially when disconnected from their prescriptive counterparts. When viewed in this way many ideas can contribute to the development of *precondition checklists* for explaining and eventually predicting the likelihood of political instability. But herein lies the strength and weakness of many qualitative explanations of political instability. Because many qualitative analysts have a message to communicate based upon ideological motives, attitudes, beliefs, and dispositions, they tend to be selective about the contents of their explanations. While the contents may be accurate as far as they go, they may miss some important elements. Similarly, qualitative analysts like Moore (1966), Wolf (1969), and Skocpol (1982) often fail to be comprehensive for a variety of analytical reasons, and where the above three focus on explanations traceable to the disenfranchised, Trimberger focuses on elite-based explanations that are equally non-comprehensive.

So how does one assess the accuracy, verifiability, and usefulness of qualitative explanatory research? The first step involves the identification of the various kinds of explanations that have been pursued by qualitative analysts. There are at least five kinds relevant to our assessment (Van Dyke 1960):

— explanations in terms of reasons;
— explanations grounded in motives, attitudes, beliefs, or dispositions;
— explanations in terms of causes;
— explanations in terms of end states; and
— explanations in terms of functions.

Explanations in terms of reasons are based upon observed events and conditions which are in turn grounded in verifiable rules about behavior. In the physical sciences, such rules are much more easily discovered than in the social sciences, but are not as easily discovered as many would have us believe. Explanations in terms of motives and dispositions are based upon the analyst's subjective view of the phenomenon under investigation. Causal explanations are distinct from reason-based ones in so far as they stress the predictability of causal events rather than rule-based behavior which may or may not predict to certain activity (like political instability). Explanations in terms of end states is aimed at producing lists of factors or variables that correlate with various kinds of instability. Functional explanations relate to the variables that explain how a system functions or fails to function. Ideally, functional explanations produce lists of factors in terms of how and to what extent they contribute to the function of the phenomenon under scrutiny.

Most of the qualitative explanations of political instability are based upon motives (like Marxist), causes, and functions, and among all of the above Skocpol is the most systematic and comprehensive. But Skocpol ignores the processes by which pre-conditions are converted into outcomes.

In addition to the comparative case study qualitative analysts are those who derive explanations of political instability from single case studies. Markides and Cohn (1982) provide a good example of a useful single case study.

The usefulness of explanatory comparative and single case studies on political instability can be assessed on two levels. First, many of the comparative case studies are useful to intelligence analysts *to the extent that they develop lists of causes and functional elements of political instability, causes and functional elements that can be used to organize and interpret intelligence according to the judgment and experience of the analyst.* But be forewarned, even Skocpol's excellent work must be treated as non-comprehensive. Consequently, intelligence analysts will have to work backwards—from the intelligence problem to the comparative case studies—to determine usefulness. Single case studies can be used in much the same way but here the level of generalization will necessarily be lower than in comparative case studies.

Comparative and single case studies can also be used in their pure forms as sources of information about political instability in specific countries or geographical regions.

Interestingly, many of the comparative and single case studies suggest (sometimes convincingly) that various factors tend to 'explain' political instability. For example, Wolf (1969) believes that peasants are the most likely participants in revolutionary movements and Migdal (1974) assigns primary responsibility to political organizations. But if an intelligence analyst was concerned about the factors that explain the instability in Iran he or she would not conduct a serious analysis without attributing a great deal of instability to religious conflict. Unfortunately, many comparative and single case studies do not attribute a great deal of explanatory influence to religious conflict, not because they believe that religious conflict is usually irrelevant to political instability analysis but because such conflict was not relevant to their particular case studies. *Intelligence analysts must thus be very careful to screen the studies they use. Better yet, they should classify them according to the kind of explanation they yield and the extent to which they are comprehensive.*

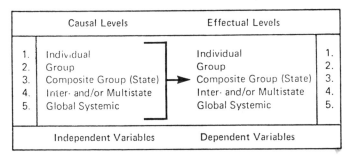

Fig. 6.1 Levels of Analysis (showing 'causal' or explanatory options, single level analysis, and multiple level analysis)

Comparative case studies are inherently less accurate than single case studies because they seek a higher level of generalization than single case studies. But single case studies are inherently less useful for the very same reason. As a general rule the higher the intended level of generalization, the lower the accuracy. Verifiability is subject to the same rule.

Implementation requirements

The use of comparative and single case studies to produce explanations of political instability is straightforward so long as one adheres to sound analytical procedures for collecting, analyzing, and interpreting empirical and subjective information. A thorough understanding of the types of explanation and levels of analysis is also desirable (Andriole 1978), as suggested in Figure 6.1. Note how the top of the figure presents the 'causal' levels of analysis as well as the levels on which we can expect to measure the 'effects' of alternative causes. The middle of the figure suggests how single causal analysis of political instability (on the state effectual level) can be conducted, while the bottom of the figure shows how multiple level analysis can be conducted. Intelligence analysts who conduct political instability analyses or contract out for such analyses should check to be sure that the analytical research design answers the levels-of-analysis question. Analyses that concentrate upon but one class of causal variables should be so classified while those that seek explanations from multiple levels should also be classified appropriately. The expertise necessary to so structure a qualitative research design is fundamental to systematic analysis.

Explanatory analysis usually takes longer to conduct than descriptive analysis because good explanations are often rooted in good descriptions. Support requirements are related to the amount of time necessary to complete the analysis; data and information requirements are similar to those required for the conduct of qualitative descriptive analysis, but analysts who seek explanations of political instability must aggregate and interpret information in ways which assure the generation of explanations based upon reasons, causes, and functions.

7 Qualitative prediction findings/methods assessment

Qualitative predictive research on political instability is at once frustrating and tantalizing. It is tantalizing because there have been some successes; but it is frustrating because the successes have not always been based upon sophisticated explanations.

We should also note that much of the qualitative predictive research conducted over the last twenty years or so has been experimental so our assessment must be tempered accordingly.

Accuracy and verifiability

Figure 7.1, from Daly and Andriole (1979), presents a view of the monitoring and warning process relevant to the assessment of political instability predictive methods and techniques. Warning here refers to four possible 'outcomes': 'hits,' 'misses,' 'false alarms,' and 'correct rejections.' Also note how the monitoring and warning process is comprised of a set of explicitly interrelated steps and sub-processes, and that no suggestion is made regarding how important each step is *vis-à-vis* the others. They are all important.

Ideally, intelligence estimates hit as frequently as possible, miss as infrequently as possible, and 'false alarm' and correctly reject what is left. The figure also suggests at least one way to assess the likelihood of political instability—the use of pattern analysis. But pattern analysis as used in this assessment refers to broad sets of activities which nearly all intelligence analysts pursue when they generate an estimate. Note also that the figure suggests that the monitoring and warning process is comprised of four preliminary steps: data collection, data screening, evaluation, and threshold setting.

The qualitative predictive methods and techniques surveyed

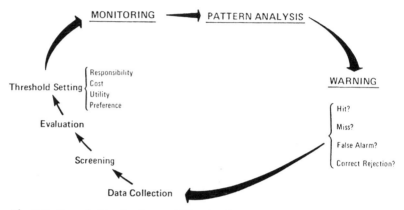

Fig. 7.1 Generic Monitoring and Warning Process

in Chapter 2 of this book can all be assessed against Figure 7.1. *But remember that ultimately the accuracy of all the qualitative predictive methods is dependent upon the accuracy of the judgments made by the experts who 'drive' the methods.* Nowhere is the old adage 'garbage in/garbage out' more appropriate; at the same time, the adage 'experience counts' is also relevant. For example, Delphi methods can be used to collect, screen, and evaluate information, set thresholds, and generate predictions impressively *if* your experts are very well qualified. The Delphi method enables experts to exchange opinions about the likelihood of events and conditions. It can be implemented by mail or direct on-site anonymous questionnaires to recognized 'experts.' More than one 'round' of judgments is always conducted and typically the experts are provided with the previous rounds' judgments as well as the rationale behind each judgment. For best results, the experts should not be assembled until the polling is completed. This will prevent the distortive influence of recognized and intimidating experts upon less notable experts and the Delphi process itself.

The Delphi method focuses forecasting opinions into an increasingly narrower range through the use of controlled feedback. The experts generally alter their prior responses somewhat when they read the responses of their colleagues. After enough rounds, the opinions usually converge into a single identifiable forecast.

Delphi predictions are useful because they exploit the

judgmental strengths of individual analysts. Delphis enable expert opinions to influence the analytical process; well designed Delphi surveys will also produce rationale for the expert judgments. Again, the method is accurate to the extent that it processes the judgments of *qualified* experts.

There are some problems with Delphi prediction, however. Because of the anonymous nature of its implementation, Delphi can generate disjointed and discontinuous predictions. It is thus sometimes difficult to produce a reliable convergence of opinions without a great deal of effort.

Many of the political risk systems discussed in Part II rely upon Delphi surveys of one kind or another. But one should be very skeptical about methods which are not completely described by their users; unfortunately, too many of the analysts and corporations that sell estimates for profit are unwilling to describe their methods in detail and those that do often undermine their own profit-making capacity by revealing methods that are far from reliable or verifiable (La Palombara 1982).

Cross-impact methods rely upon subjective assessments of how events and conditions co-vary predictively. The main strength of the cross-impact method is that it allows forecasters to estimate the likelihood of events or conditions based upon the likelihood of other events or conditions. Like all of the qualitative forecasting methods, the cross-impact method is only as diagnostic as the estimates which fuel its use.

In terms of Figure 7.1, cross-impact methods are less likely to contribute to monitoring and warning than the other methods discussed thus far *because cross-impact methods force analysts to concentrate on the interrelationships among predictive variables rather than upon the primary object of the predictive analysis.*

Still another subjective predictive methodology relies upon the use of *Bayes' theorem of conditional probabilities.* The three variations of Bayesian forecasting discussed in Chapter 2 include simple Bayesian updating, probability or influence diagramming, and hierarchical inference structuring. At the core of all three variations is the use of Bayes' theorem for revising a probability in the light of new information.

All of the Bayesian, or probabilistic, methods facilitate the use of many different kinds of experts. Moreover, because the methods are subjective, they are explicit. (However, the Bayesian methods can be tedious. Consequently, computer support is almost always necessary to implement them productively.) *They remain popular primarily because many managers and analysts still distrust heavily empirical analyses and because whatever the forecast it is traceable before, during, and after its issue.*

The three applied Bayesian methods all rely upon subjective or 'expert' judgments and probability estimates. Bayes' theorem of conditional probabilities is implemented rather easily while hierarchical inference structuring is relatively difficult to use. However, since all of the Bayesian methods have been computerized (Andriole 1981), they can all be implemented effectively, given enough relative time, talent, and support.

The hierarchical inference structuring technique deserves very special mention. It is perfectly suited to the intelligence requirements suggested in Figure 7.1. It also facilitates the focusing of different expert opinions at different parts of the predictive problem. This aspect, in turn, encourages group prediction by exposing the many and varied components of a complicated predictive problem. To our knowledge, the hierarchical inference technique has yet to be applied to the political instability prediction problem. We believe that an experiment in this area would prove very productive.

Our optimism is based upon *the successful use of the technique for international forecasting (Andriole 1981) and—most importantly—because it permits the integration of subjective and empirical data* in ways that other subjective or objective methods do not. Specifically, because the hierarchical inference structuring method requires the analyst to model the problem according to his or her best judgment (and the judgment of his or her colleagues) *before* the assessment of current intelligence takes place, analysts can spend as much time as necessary front-ending the predictive problem and then be in a position to process intelligence quickly and efficiently as it is gathered.

Unfortunately, there are hardly any verifications of any of the subjective methods and the few that have been conducted suggest that experts have biases that can affect their predictive performance. There is also evidence that suggests that quantitative statistical predictive models outperform qualitative ones *for certain kinds of predictive problems.* Is political instability prediction akin to sales predictions or predictions of OPEC intentions? The recalcitrance of the OPEC intentions problem is clearly greater than the sales problem, suggesting that qualitative methods may be more productive than quantitative ones for solving such problems. Until more experiments are conducted we cannot know what kind of a problem we are dealing with.

Finally, assessments about the utility of qualitative predictive methods and techniques (note that there are very few 'findings') should be based to some extent upon the goals and objects of prediction for which the methods are best suited. Predictive goals may be distinguished according to their ranges. There are short-range predictions, medium-range predictions, long-range predictions, and even retrospective predictions. Unfortunately, there is no common definition about what constitutes a short-range versus long-range prediction. To some a short-range prediction extends out sixty days or less. Many others regard one year as a short-range prediction. In the business community, for example, a long-range prediction is generally one which extends no further than three years in time. But in the intelligence community a long-range prediction may extend well beyond twenty years into the future.

In addition to short, medium, and long-range prediction ranges, problem-solvers should also distinguish between positive and negative predictive goals. Positive and negative predictions are concerned with what will and with what will not happen, respectively. Finally, problem-solvers should distinguish between objective and normative predictions. Objective predictions present what will be, while normative ones suggest what ought to be.

Most problems require predictions that are objective, positive, and short-range in nature. When information is sparse, or talent unavailable, negative and retrospective prediction may be used to enhance more positive future-oriented ones. Normative prediction is more frequently the preoccupation of planners.

Intelligence analyses and estimates about the likelihood of political instability are usually short-range, or up to one year into the future. This is the case because available qualitative and quantitative methods are generally only credible when they yield short-range predictions, and because the intelligence community is usually most interested in short-range predictions.

The intelligence community is also most interested in positive objective prediction, or what is likely to happen instead of what will—or should—not happen. All of the qualitative prediction methods that are discussed in this book are unquestionably best suited to short-range, positive prediction, although Delphi can be adapted to produce short-range negative predictions. Methodological assessments should also distinguish among possible prediction objects. For example, event prediction is by definition and nature more specific and precise than the prediction of conditions. It is also important to distinguish between events and conditions which occur within or outside of the particular environments which are the objects of prediction.

Accordingly, political instability prediction assessments should include assessments about predictive goals *and* objects.

Implementation requirements

The Delphi method can be complicated to implement, especially when the number of participants is large. Questionnaires must be designed, reproduced, and mailed out or personally distributed. Frequently the participants do not return the questionnaires on time. Questionnaires also sometimes come back filled out improperly or incompletely. Considerable support is also necessary to analyze and compute the responses.

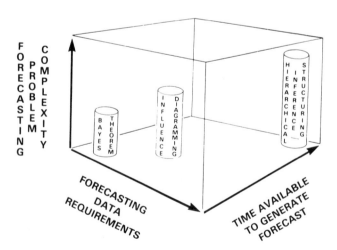

Fig. 7.2 Bayesian Forecasting Method Requirements

Other problems include the difficulty of finding enough appropriate experts, developing a sophisticated questionnaire, and reifying the results of the questionnaire.

Cross-impact analyses are also time-consuming and require a good deal of predictive problem structuring expertise. Unlike the Delphi method, however, the cross-impact method is almost always computer-based.

Bayesian methods may be distinguished according to their support requirements, as Figure 7.2 suggests. But fortunately all of the Bayesian techniques have been computerized. We must stress, however, that a good deal of expertise is required to implement the Bayesian methods. In the past, users have been disappointed with the use of Bayesian methods not always because of methodological issues, but because they were unskilled in the most fundamental aspects of the methodology.

8 Quantitative description findings/methods assessment

The quantitative research surveyed in Part II focused upon the development of empirical definitions of instability, empirical distinctions among political instability, political crises, and revolution, event data-based definitions of instability, quantitative indicators of instability, 'internal situation profiles,' and the assembly of quantitative empirical data bases on political instability. But how useful is the work?

Accuracy and verifiability

It is difficult to assess the utility of competing qualitative *or* quantitative definitions of political instability. In many ways the problem is similar to selecting a new car from several manufacturers and many models. On the most general level, all of them have similar safety features, use a petroleum-based fuel, and are reasonably reliable. The choice thus often reduces to questions of size, color, and comfort. The evaluation and selection of definitions of political instability similarly often reduce to personal analytical preferences.

For example, quantitative distinctions among internal war, rebellion, collective protest, and the like are often drawn *after* empirical data is gathered and analyzed. Rummel (1963), for example, conducts a complicated factor analysis of political instability and then labels the dimensions of instability, not according to theoretical notions about instability, but according to what the statistical operation suggested was appropriate. Such descriptive research is often referred to as 'barefoot empiricism' and is only slightly useful to the intelligence analyst responsible for describing instability in ways which will accelerate the analysis and estimating process.

The methodological issues connected with excessive quantitative empirical measurements are also by no means clearly understood. Debate rages on *among the practitioners* about what constitutes proper measurement.

Much less sophisticated are event data-based definitions of political instability. Most of this research can be reduced to equating political instability to numbers of domestic conflict events: 16 assassination attempts, 6 riots, and 14 strikes = instability, but 1 assassination attempt, 2 riots, and 6 strikes ≠ instability. For substantive political instability analysts the notion of counting to determine whether or not a country is unstable seems silly—and rightly so. It must be remembered that the efforts to quantify domestic conflict events were launched in order to facilitate the use of correlation and regression techniques—not to develop new conceptualizations of political instability.

Relatedly, Spector's (1975) work to develop general quantitative indicators of political instability extends the counting logic and presumes—like much of the quantitative work—that patterns of political instability behavior exist, patterns that more or less apply cross-nationally. The intelligence analyst of course has an altogether different working premise. He or she assumes that instability in El Salvador is substantively very different from that which has occurred in Iran. Suggestions to generalize—even on a purely descriptive level—across the El Salvadoran and Iranian cases would probably be regarded as bizarre and dangerous. Our view is that, for example, event data-based and other quantitative indicators are not yet ready to be used by the intelligence community—and may never be because of competing analytical perspectives and because quantitative research is so plagued by methodological problems that even when it actually describes, explains, or predicts phenomena, its proponents are frequently not completely sure how or why it does so.

On the other hand, there are more modest quantitative attempts to describe domestic events and conditions that may be potentially useful to intelligence analysts. One example is the Internal Situational Profile (ISP), developed experimentally by Hopple (1978). The ISP is potentially useful because it relies upon raw data, that is, data that has not been elaborately converted or force-fitted into an arbitrary concept. The indicators used to monitor changes in the domestic condition of a country are very straightforward and intuitively diagnostic of domestic change. The ISP idea has yet to be fully studied but several advantages come to mind even at this early stage of its development:

— ISP indicators can be used as is, added to, deleted, or modified according to the analyst's preferences and needs;
— ISP results stress change; and
— ISPs are relatively easy to develop, interpret, compare, and integrate into other intelligence analyses and estimates.

The strength of the ISP method lies in its simplicity and flexibility. In many respects ISPs are the result of the very first steps taken by quantitative analysts who usually have their sights set on the conduct of multiple regression analyses. ISPs stop far short of such analyses and simultaneously discard the assumptions inherent in aggregate cross-national analysis.

Not unlike the ISP approach are those which attempt to develop distributions of domestic violence over time. Gurr and Bishop (1976), for example, categorize domestic violence and then search for its occurrence through history. *If you accept their definitions then you may find their tour interesting but probably of little applied value because broadbrush looks at any phenomena are generally more useful to theorists than practitioners.*

Assessments about the accuracy and verifiability of quantitative descriptive research must be based upon the purpose(s) at which the quantification is targeted. Much of the quantitative descriptive research on political instability is intended to play a small part in a larger quantitative effort, while other research, like the development of ISPs, is intended to stand alone. Quantitative descriptions are thus accurate in the minds of many if they facilitate more sophisticated analyses or contribute to a larger body of quantitative analysis also intended to facilitate additional quantification. In other words, many quantitative analysts collect data about domestic violence and look for descriptive groupings and patterns without regard for individual country contexts or specific applied requirements. Moreover, independent of purposes, some of the quantitative descriptive data is incomplete and unreliable. Event data, for example, extracted from the *New York Times*, London *Times*, or

The Guardian does not measure domestic violence but rather what the public sources report and interpret as domestic violence. Source coverage studies have repeatedly illustrated that reporting biases greatly affect the development of event data bases. Indicators developed from biased and incomplete data can only yield biased and incomplete descriptions. This rule holds true for the development of quantitative definitions, indicators, and typologies.

Implementation requirements

If you would like to develop quantitative definitions, indicators, and/or typologies of political instability you should have a good deal of expertise in concept formation, data collection, and measurement. Your concepts must be valid, that is, grounded in observable reality, before any data is collected. If the data to be collected is in any way affected by the collection process, then data reliability measures must be developed and applied. Reliable data must also be available. Expertise in the use of descriptive or summary statistics is another prerequisite.

Quantitative empirical data is also very expensive to collect and usually takes a lot more time to assemble than planned. Support in the form of data collectors and computer time is also necessary.

9 Quantitative explanation findings/methods assessment

An enormous amount of quantitative explanatory research has been conducted during the last twenty years. Most of it has attempted to link 'determinants' with political instability via hypotheses that contain one or more determinant or 'independent' variables. Causal models have also been used to explain political instability.

Accuracy and verifiability

The assessment watchword for quantitative explanatory research is diversity. Some analysts look for internal explanations of instability while others look for explanations in the international or global environments. The list of internal determinants includes economic, social, political, elite, and mass psychological factors; international and global ones include economic and political 'penetration,' the contagious effect of conflict, and war. The causal modelers have frequently attempted to include a little bit of everything in their research.

Given all of this effort, what has been learned about political instability?

- Lichbach and Gurr (1981) demonstrated that sometimes past rebellion leads to future rebellions.
- Fenmore and Volgy (1978) demonstrated that short-term economic change is related to political instability.
- Hibbs (1973) demonstrated that low rates of economic growth explain high levels of instability; but Eckstein (1980) refuted the conclusion.
- Midlarsky (1982) demonstrated that instability is related to socio-economic inequality.

- Huntington (1968) found that modernization leads to instability but Sigelman (1979) found that Huntington was 'wrong'.
- Gurr (1974b) found that Huntington's notions of political institutionalization and stability were also 'wrong'.
- Nearly all of the quantitative studies on the impact of governmental performance are inconclusive.
- The use of mass psychological variables (relative deprivation, and the like) to explain instability has yielded cries of outrage, contradictory results, and a paucity of findings.
- Elite-based explanations of instability have been inconclusive.
- Outside economic variables—like penetration—tend to explain aspects of political instability.
- And causal models of political instability have probably confused the analytical process more than they have clarified it, especially from an applied perspective.

How should we assess the above? First, if usefulness is traceable to consistently replicated research then very little of the above is useful to intelligence analysis. But the larger issue concerns the caveats which apply to *all* quantitative empirical research, caveats which are related to concepts, data sources, data reliability, data availability, hypothesis formation, time periods, data and variable aggregation, statistical operations, and statistical significance, just to name a few areas that can undermine a quantitative analysis. *Such problems suggest that a utility assessment of quantitative explanatory research findings is extremely premature.* In fact, we would argue that quantitative explanatory research is still very much in its infancy.

But this does not mean that intelligence analysts will find nothing of value in the *processes* by which quantitative explanatory research is conducted. First, *the exercises which lead to the formation of hypotheses are useful to intelligence analysts if for no other than inventory purposes.* While the results of quantitative research may be unimpressive, quantitative analysts are often very thorough and sometimes highly imaginative when it comes to identifying potential 'causes' of instability. *We recommend that attention be paid to the exercises which identify possible determinants of political instability; we also suggest that some time be spent looking at the strength and direction of some of the relationships discovered by quantitative analysts.* While a multitude of factors (caveats?) may have contributed to a given relationship, especially *strong ones can be used to rank potentially useful determinants, while very weak ones can be ignored altogether.*

It is also important to remember that the quantitative explanatory studies discussed in Part II are all targeted at the generation of *partial explanations* of instability (Kaplan 1964), which are essential parts of the knowledge production process but of relatively little—and sometimes misleading—use to intelligence analysts. Here again the distinctions among those who strive to produce knowledge and those who strive to apply it are very evident. A partial explanation of instability may be exciting to a theorist but frustrating to an intelligence analyst who cannot know if the key determinant is presented in the quantitative analysis or was left out simply because it was unrelated to the hypothesis in question.

Finally, nearly all of the quantitative analyses in this survey use aggregate data and many 'cases' to test their explanatory hypotheses. Consequently, cases which are the exception to the aggregate rule are lost, cases which may be the most useful to the intelligence analyst *because they are unique.* Unfortunately, the statistical and behavioral research assumptions which define quantitative analysis are at odds with the requirements of the intelligence community, which is seldom heard requesting information about the general causes of instability in highly industrialized societies, but would rather hear about the likelihood of a Saudi collapse. *To the extent that these goals are different, aggregate cross-national quantitative explanatory analysis is incompatible with intelligence analysis.*

Implementation requirements

It is perhaps not surprising that a struggling sub-field of political instability research requires more expertise, time, data, and support than one which has a more impressive history. But be aware that the proper conduct of quantitative explanatory research requires expertise in the substance of political instability *and* quantitative analytical methodologies like correlation, regression, and causal modeling. It also requires a great deal of reliable data, support, and time. Even though many of the statistical procedures have been computerized in batch or interactive programs like SPSS (Statistical Package for the Social Sciences), one must know what procedures to use and how to interpret statistical results. We must also point out that investments in quantitative explanatory analyses are not likely to yield many applied pay-offs, at least not in the immediate future. There are just too many methodological issues to be settled before any real applied progress can be made.

10 Quantitative prediction findings/methods assessment

Attempts to predict political instability via quantitative methodology have been few and disappointing: if it is safe to say that quantitative explanatory research is still in its infancy then quantitative predictive research on political instability is still gestating.

Accuracy and verifiability

A discussion of the accuracy and verifiability of quantitative predictive research is obviously premature. For example, all event data-based predictive research has been inconclusive. Largely based upon persistence models of behavior, which simply state that what has happened in the immediate past is likely to affect what happens in the immediate future, these event data (computerized) systems have not been evaluated systematically (Andriole and Hopple 1981). At the same time, there was some research that suggested that events can be used to monitor and predict events in Japan and Peru, but this research is very tentative. Moreover, there are so many conceptual and methodological problems connected with the use of event data that applied predictive opportunities are very, very few.

Leading indicators have also been used to predict intranational events and conditions, but not too successfully (Abolfathi *et al.* 1980). Yet the *quantitative predictive case study approach* used by Abolfathi and his associates is certainly more promising than event data-based approaches. The case study approach recognizes that cross-national prediction may miss a lot of unusual activity buried in the aggregate data. Indicators derived from detailed case studies can be useful *if* tested and verified. Two serious problems exist, however. The first has to do with the number of indicators included in the predictive analysis. How do you know when you have enough or too many? The second problem is more serious. When indicators 'lead' or 'lag' instability we have no way of knowing *why* they are moving. The use of indicators is validated when they consistently correlate with instability, *not when predictive rationales are satisfied* by the occurrence or non-occurrence of political instability. In the intelligence community the estimates that are the most credible are generally those that can be defended convincingly. Quantitative indicators might thus be used by intelligence analysts as *triggers or alerting devices which might then be used to organize the search for predictive rationale.* But remember that we are still a long way from the development and application of reliable quantitative indicators.

Causal models have also been used to predict instability but here too the results have been unimpressive (Gurr and Lichbach 1979). Even Dahlgren's (1976, 1978) attempt to use Gurr's causal model with expert judgments failed to generate any real analytical enthusiasm. In general, causal models are so large and complex that frequently even the modelers have no idea what will be discovered. In other words, causal models are often used as catch-all tools for assessing as many inter-relationships as possible. The results are then used to refine the initial causal model. This process may be repeated again and again until the model is refined as much as it can be. But again, at this point in time the use of causal models to predict political instability should be confined to basic researchers.

While interesting, the use of simulation to predict instability is also a basic research enterprise. (Part II discusses some of the issues connected with the use of simulation for prediction.)

Implementation requirements

Considerable statistical expertise is necessary to implement indicator, causal model, and simulation-based predictive research; substantial substantive knowledge is also required so that meaningful predictive research can be conducted. Data requirements are also large. Computer support is necessary as well. Finally, the use of quantitative predictive methods and techniques is also very time-consuming.

Summary and conclusions

As Figure S.1 suggests, this assessment is grounded in a survey of *qualitative and quantitative descriptive, explanatory, and predictive political instability research*. The research in the survey covers the period from around 1960 to 1983. The assessment itself is grounded in *two general evaluative criteria: accuracy-and-verifiability and implementation requirements*.

The survey attempts to identify research that describes the events and conditions that characterize political instability and revolution. The explanatory research in the survey is concerned with the factors or 'variables' that explain political instability and revolution, that is, which can be associated with the occurrence of instability. The predictive research seeks to identify the factors likely to precede and therefore 'predict to' the occurrence of instability.

The distinction between qualitative and quantitative research drawn in this book is one which regards qualitative research as that which relies principally upon the collection and organization of subjective or 'expert' data, while quantitative research is that which relies upon the use of the 'scientific methods.' Qualitative research is usually characterized by the use of historical and case study approaches; quantitative research is often grounded in the formulation of hypotheses, the conversion of 'soft' concepts into numerical form, and the testing of hypotheses via some kind of statistical analysis.

The criteria of accuracy-and-verifiability and implementation requirements are defined in terms of objectivity and the requirements necessary to use the methods discussed in the survey. Objectivity is traceable to the replication of analytical results, while the implementation requirements are traceable to the amount of expertise, time, data, and support necessary for serious use.

The *qualitative descriptive research* presented in the survey focuses on *case studies* of specific political instability and revolutions; *definitions* of political instability usually grounded in definitions of collective action; *classifications* of political instability; *typologies* of political instability and revolutions; and *stages* through which instability and revolution can be expected to pass.

Qualitative explanatory research includes explanations of instability grounded in history and sociology (frequently based upon a comparative case study approach); explanations attributable to the behavior of peasant, agrarian, and otherwise disenfranchised classes in society; explanations attributable to elite behavior; and explanations attributable to political structure, social movements, ethnicity, and terrorism.

Qualitative predictive research concentrates upon identifying the factors that can be expected to lead to political instability and revolution via the use of intuition; Delphi forecasting; cross-impact forecasting; and Bayesian forecasting. These subjective methods can be characterized as *systematic* (with the exception of intuition), that is, those that help with the organization and processing of subjective or expert judgments. Delphi forecasting involves polling experts in multiple 'rounds' until a consensus forecast is generated. Cross-impact forecasting requires the analyst to consider the predictive impact of one event upon sets of others. Bayesian methods are based upon the use of Bayes' theorem of conditional probabilities, a formula for assessing the impact of new information upon prior odds or probabilities. There are three varieties of Bayesian forecasting presented in the book: the simple use of Bayes' theorem for probability updating, the use of influence diagrams, and the use of hierarchical inference structuring. Influence diagramming involves stringing together the events likely to predict the occurrence or non-occurrence of instability; hierarchical inference structuring involves identifying and arranging the data, indicators, and activities likely to precede instability according to expert ideas about how the factors all interrelate.

Quantitative descriptive research involves *definitions* of political instability *grounded in empirical 'counts'* of various conflictual events and conditions; the development of *empirical definitions of and distinctions among* 'political instability,' 'political crisis,' 'collective political violence,' 'rebellion,'

Methods / Foci	Qualitative	Quantitative
DESCRIPTION		
EXPLANATION	Political Instability Research Survey, 1960–1983	
PREDICTION		

Criteria / Methods	Accuracy & Verifiability	Implementation Requirements
QUALITATIVE DESCRIPTIVE		
QUALITATIVE EXPLANATORY		
QUALITATIVE PREDICTIVE	Assessments In Connection With Intelligence Analysis And Estimates	
QUANTITATIVE DESCRIPTIVE		
QUANTITATIVE EXPLANATORY		
QUANTITATIVE PREDICTIVE		

Fig. S.1 Organization of Research Survey and Methodological Assessment

and 'protest'; the development of *quantitative indicators* of instability; the development of *computer-based 'early warning and monitoring systems'* grounded in domestic event data; the development of *governmental change indices*; the development of *Internal Situation Profiles*; and quantitative descriptions of *terrorist-induced instability*.

Quantitative explanatory research has focused upon intra-national and international 'causes' of political instability and revolution. *Intranational* causes include economic factors, like short-term economic change, modernization, and economic growth rate; social factors, like 'cleavage' within society, structural imbalances, and the degree to which a society is modernized; political factors like the level of democratization and the persistence and durability of the political system; aggregate psychological factors, like 'relative deprivation' and perceptions about violence; and elite factors, like elite-inspired coups, repression, and elite-based terrorism. *International* factors include the effect of 'diffusion' and 'contagion' and the impact of foreign economic and political penetration. Nearly all of this work attempts to quantify the factors listed above and then test hypotheses statistically about how the factors co-vary, if at all.

Quantitative predictive research is less voluminous and successful than nearly all of the categories covered in this book. The event data-based systems for 'forecasting' intra-national conflict, causal models of political instability, and simulations are all highly experimental at this point in time.

The assessment of the usefulness to intelligence analysts of the above research in political instability is directed exclusively at the production of intelligence analyses and estimates. No attempt is made in this book to suggest how improvements in the integration of intelligence can be made. No suggestions about how the intelligence community should be organized are made.

First, it is important to not only understand the differences between qualitative and quantitative research methodologies and findings but the alternative ways that they can be used in political instability intelligence analysis as well. Generally speaking, *and given the structure and organization of the intelligence community*, qualitative analyses which concentrate upon individual countries, regions, political parties, religious organizations, and the like, are much more likely to be integrated into the intelligence production process than cross-national aggregate data analyses. In our view, this is likely to be the case regardless of the quality of the qualitative or quantitative analyses in question.

Qualitative analyses and findings are also more likely to

be influential because they use the methods that are the most widely used and understood in the intelligence community. We would also argue that qualitative political instability research findings and analyses have been more accurate than quantitative ones, so long as 'accuracy' is understood as consistency and relative clarity.

The problem with most quantitative analyses as we see them is, first, their lack of substance. Many quantitative descriptive, explanatory, and predictive analyses are not uninformed by theoretical insight but they are sadly lacking in the 'stuff' of the intranational politics they are trying to describe, explain, and predict. Secondly, quantitative analysts have yet to get their methodological house in order. There is still angry debate about even the most basic methodological issues. The sources and reliability of data remain serious problems, as does the tendency to generalize on the basis of a large number of *disparate* 'cases' across various points in time. An even more serious methodological problem is the variance that can be produced in one's quantitative results by varying even the smallest methodological components of one's analysis. *A change in data groupings, time periods (for example, yearly versus monthly periods), and data sources can completely alter the results of analyses of the same basic phenomena.* Related to this problem is the statistical model that performs perfectly, but because of theoretical and substantive anemia, says very little about instability.

A third general problem revealed in our survey and assessment concerns the partial nature of many quantitative studies and analyses. The problem arises when a quantitative analysis is presented as a piece of finished research when in reality it is merely a tiny step in a long, long journey. On the other end of the interpretive continuum is the complex model which defies disentanglement to the point where it is impossible to attribute analytical influence to any of the variables within the model.

Yet another problem with much of the quantitative research can be found in the motivations and goals of the analysts themselves and the analytical requirements of the research 'consumers'. Traditional analysts have from the beginning attempted to influence analysis and practice while quantitative ones often attempt to develop empirical theory. Traditional analysts seek to change through study, insight, wisdom, and intuition; quantitative empiricists try to demonstrate, test, and ultimately 'prove' their hypotheses about the way nations act and interact, regardless of possible applied implications.

But perhaps more serious is the possibility that trends and patterns about political instability are undiscoverable because they do not exist. In other words, if it is the case that the recalcitrance of political instability defies any systematic study aimed at developing generalizable propositions and theories, then the quantitative analysis of political instability is likely to remain pretty much where it is today. Those who believe that patterns and trends of political instability activity cannot be discovered believe that all cases are unique; those who believe that patterns and trends can be discovered believe that there are similarities across cases. But even if there are, we have already argued that cross-national generalities about political instability are much less useful to intelligence analysts than information about particular countries, groups, and political systems.

This 'attack' upon quantitative-empirical cross-national political research is *not* to suggest that there is nothing useful in the quantitative search for patterns and trends or that qualitative research is in any respect foolproof. Many have warned about the biases inherent in subjective data, about the problems connected with treating subjective information as discrete and (for example, during Bayesian analysis) equally important. Many qualitative analyses are also overtly normative. This is particularly true of the analyses conducted by qualitative philosophers, social engineering theorists, and ideologues of one persuasion or another. Intelligence analysts should thus be careful to distinguish between objective and normative qualitative analyses.

The structured qualitative techniques (Delphi, cross-impact, Bayesian) can help a great deal in lending order and some precision to qualitative analysis but here one must be extremely diligent about the selection of 'experts,' who under normal conditions will disagree as often as they agree.

Quantitative research can be used by intelligence analysts in the following ways:

— Cross-national quantitative definitions of political instability

can be used to suggest ways to conceptualize specific national
and regional definitions *and* to 'check' existing applied
definitions.

— Quantitative indicators of political instability can be used to
supplement applied indicator lists and suggest how indicators
can be integrated into individual country lists or rejected.

— Quantitative Internal Situation Profiles (ISPs) and similar
unsophisticated indicator systems can be used to organize
and monitor internal political processes especially when
integrated with *experienced judgments* about how to interpret changes in the indicators and larger ISP.

— Quantitative explanatory research can help with the assessment of determinants of political instability that traditional
analysts undertake on a routine basis; highly correlated
determinants—while almost always non-comprehensive—
can be scrutinized a little more carefully than uncorrelated
ones.

— Quantitative explanatory research can be used to develop
inventories of indicators, determinants, and other factors
that have been empirically linked with political instability,
inventories that can then be used to develop lists of determinants for individual countries and/or regions. These
lists would of course have to be compiled by country analysts;
the strength of the empirical relationships—because of
countless methodological and other problems—would *not*
alone be enough to 'admit' an indicator into an active indicator group.

— The processes of problem structuring which are indigenous
to scientific problem-solving can inform some analytical
activities; scientific problem-structuring frequently involves
concept formation, data collection, hypothesis construction,
and modeling. These processes can be of help to those who
must formulate the right questions, reformulate the old ones,
and avoid at all costs those questions unrelated to the problem at hand.

— The information, or data, management aspect of quantitative
research is also potentially valuable to analysts. Information
collection, storage, retrieval, analysis and display are all useful
—especially when computer-based in interactive management systems. Since frequently 'institutional memory' is confined to but a few individuals, computer-based information

management can provide immediate feedback to users who need to retrieve past and analyze current information.

This assessment of political instability research methodologies favors the use of qualitative methods over purely quantitative ones. But this is not to say that *all* qualitative methods are useful or that the results of qualitative analyses are always relevant to political instability intelligence analysis and estimating. In fact, a strong case can be made that the qualitative analyses that have been conducted have been largely unsystematic, and that some of the more promising qualitative methods have been underutilized. Nevertheless, the useful methods and findings are as follows:

— Qualitative case studies of specific instances of political instability, revolution, and domestic crisis can be useful to an analyst engaged in similar analyses.
— Qualitative high and low-level generalizations, when verifiable by an analyst's experience, judgment, and wisdom, can be applied to real-world analysis on a country or regional basis, but generalizations that extend beyond countries or regions should be very carefully scrutinized.
— Qualitative definitions and classifications of political instability can be used productively when passed through a set of situational filters.
— Stages of revolution grounded in qualitative analysis are useful—*when modified* for specific country application—as descriptive or monitoring tools.
— Qualitative normative explanations of political instability should be 'objectivized' before use; some normative concepts, notions, and theories can help with the analysis of individual instances of instability as well as interpretations of the motivations of revolutionary leaders.
— Objective qualitative explanatory analyses can be used to develop pre-instability checklists, although such checklists should be regarded as non-comprehensive.
— Delphi, cross-impact, and Bayesian predictive methods can lend order and precision to qualitative analyses.
— Bayesian, Delphi, and cross-impact methods exploit the expertise of analysts, the uniqueness of instability events and conditions, and the strength of group forecasting.
— And hierarchical inference structuring, which involves

identifying the 'preferred options' or undefined expected utility of 'perpetrators,' can be used to organize and 'solve' instability problems; this method is perhaps the strongest one identified in this survey and assessment because it permits the focusing of different expertise at a single problem. It also permits the integration of quantitative empirical research in a way unlike nearly all other hybrid alternatives.

Notes

1. Space limitations force us to condense what could be an extended treatise into a few paragraphs. Orlansky (1970) discusses many of the common 'typologies' of 'internal war.'
2. There are also many quantitatively derived typologies. These are discussed in the section on quantitative description.
3. We discuss the quantitative explanatory internal conflict–external conflict research in Part II. Since the work has by and large been unproductive, our discussion will be brief.
4. How to fit terrorism into an instability review is a problem. We treat certain forms of terrorism as an elite phenomenon (because the nihilistic/chiliastic/ideological terrorists such as the Japanese Red Army and the Italian Red Brigades are small and elitist sects and should be analyzed with the perspectives and tools used to study political elites) and therefore briefly discuss such terrorism in Part II. 'Mass terrorism,' which usually occurs in the context of internal war or revolution (see Thornton 1964), represents one of many collective violence strategies. It may be used frequently (the FLN in Algeria), selectively (the Vietcong in Vietnam), intermittently (the ELF in Ethiopia), or as a substitute for armed insurrection and other tactics on the internal war menu (the IRA in Northern Ireland).
5. Relative deprivation means roughly what it says, that people may feel deprived in a relative sense (because they see a frustrating gap between what they want and what they get). The concept is discussed in detail in Part II.
6. But we must attach a caveat to our caveat. Most of the relevant research comes from university students and artificial laboratory situations. For two very useful correctives, see Christensen-Szalanski and Bushyhead (1981) and Hogarth (1981).
7. When risk experts rank countries for potential instability, the lists can show little or no overlap. For example, see *Business Week* (1980).
8. Social mobilization refers to the upsurge in societal activity which occurs as part of the modernization process. Old values and behaviors break down and are replaced by new ones. This concept is important to many theories of political instability, although it is rarely measured precisely or even directly.

9. Similarly, Gurr's (1970) model is designed to apply to all regions. Welfling (1975) unearths some different patterns for Africa, and Cooper (1974), who reassesses relationships within five cultural and three modernity groups, is able to improve the predictions of Gurr's model of 'turmoil' significantly. Cooper also identifies some patterns unique to particular types of nations.

10. In an interesting application, Cuzan and Heggen (1982) use their approach to 'explain' the 1979 Nicaraguan revolution.

11. Some refer to CAT as the resource mobilization, or RM, perspective (McCarthy and Zald 1977; Synder 1978).

12. Mass psychological characteristics include beliefs and values as well as personality traits and psychoanalytical processes. The emphasis is on what people *believe* and *perceive*, not the less direct personality traits and processes.

13. Unless terrorism is used as part of a revolutionary strategy—as in the case of the FLN in Algeria—or is resorted to intermittently, as illustrated by the Eritrean Liberation Front in Ethiopia—along with other techniques of rebellion.

14. Markides and Cohn (1982), discussed briefly in Chapter 2, look in detail at the Cyprus case and come up with some additional conditions for the idea that external conflict leads to internal cohesion.

15. On the Japan project, see Spector *et al.* (1975). The Peru project is covered in Slater and Orloski (1978).

16. A brief digression: intelligence analysts need the least help for case studies, which is what they do the best.

17. Examples abound. Especially dangerous is the situation where two indicators are very closely but not genuinely related. For example, a background factor may actually be causing both. Instead of X causing Y, Z is causing X and Y. There is a very strong link between the number of fire trucks at a fire and the damage resulting, but not because they are causally tied together—a third factor, the size of the fire, is really accounting for both of them. Causal modeling, with its emphasis on causal paths and direct and indirect effects, is of value for the reason that it forces the analyst to really think about webs of relationships (although not always successfully).

18. Simulation is a method which recreates the central features of reality in a simplified context. Simulation may be based on human inputs, man-machine combined inputs, or all-machine or computer-based models. Rastogi's model, like many of the more recent ones, is a complex, fully computerized one.

References

Abolfathi, F., S. Becker, K. Feste, J. Husbands, and D. McCormick (1980), *Developing Indicators of Political Instability in Less Developed Countries: A Feasibility Study*, 3 volumes, Arlington VA, CACI, Inc.

Adas, M. (1979), *Prophets of Rebellion*, Chapel Hill, NC, University of North Carolina Press.

Al-Abdin, A. Z. (1979), 'The Free Yemeni Movement (1940-48) and Its Ideas on Reform,' *Middle East Studies* 15: 36-48.

Allan, P. and A. A. Stahel (1983), 'Tribal Guerrilla Warfare Against a Colonial Power: Analyzing the War in Afghanistan,' *Journal of Conflict Resolution* 27 (December): 590-617.

Andriole, S. J. (1976), 'Progress Report on the Development of an Integrated Crisis Warning System,' Technical Report 76-19, December, McLean, VA, Decisions and Designs, Inc.

Andriole, S. J. (1978), 'The Levels of Analysis Problem and the Study of Foreign, International, and Global Affairs,' *International Interactions* 5: 113-33.

Andriole, S. J. (1979), 'Decision Process Models and the Needs of Policy Makers: Thoughts on the Foreign Policy Interface,' *Policy Sciences* 11: 19-37.

Andriole, S. J. (1981), 'Computer-Based Bayesian Forecasting Methodologies,' in G. W. Hopple and J. A. Kuhlman (eds), *Expert-Generated Data: Applications in International Affairs*, Boulder, CO, Westview.

Andriole, S. J. (1983), *Handbook of Problem Solving: An Analytical Methodology*, Princeton, NJ, Petrocelli.

Andriole, S. J. and G. W. Hopple (1981), *The Rise and Fall of Event Data: Thoughts on an Incomplete Journey From Basic Research to Applied Use in the U.S. Department of Defense*, Marshall, VA, International Information Systems, Inc.

Andriole, S. J. and R. A. Young (1977), 'Toward the Development of an Integrated Crisis Warning System,' *International Studies Quarterly* 21 (March): 107-50.

Aya, R. (1979), 'Theories of Revolution Reconsidered,' *Theory and Society* 8 (July): 39-99.

Barclay, S., C. Peterson, C. Kelly, L. Phillips, and J. Selvidge (1977), *Handbook for Decision Analysis*, McLean, VA, Decisions and Designs, Inc.

Barnes, S. H., M. Kaase, *et al.* (1979), *Political Action*, Beverly Hills, CA, Sage.

Belden, T. (1977), 'Indications, Warning, and Crisis Operations,' *International Studies Quarterly* **21**, 1: 181-98.

Bell, J. B. (1974), 'Endemic Insurgency and International Order: The Eritrean Experience,' *Orbis* **17**: 427-50.

Booz, Allen and Hamilton (1981), 'Political Instability in LDCs,' Final Report, 15 January, Bethesda, MD, Booz, Allen, & Hamilton, Inc.

Boulding, E. (1979), 'Ethnic Separatism and World Development,' pp. 259-81 in L. Kriesberg (ed.), *Research in Social Movements, Conflict, and Change*, Vol. II, Greenwich, CT, JAI Press.

Brinton, C. (1938), *The Anatomy of Revolution*, Englewood Cliffs, NJ, Prentice-Hall.

Bueno de Mesquita, B. (1981), *The War Trap*, New Haven, CT, Yale.

Business Week (1980), 'Foreign Investment: The Post-Shah Surge in Political Risk Studies,' 1 December.

Carroll, M. P. (1975), 'Revitalization Movements and Social Structure,' *American Sociological Review* **4** (June): 398-401.

Chan, S. (1979), 'The Intelligence of Stupidity: Understanding Failures in Strategic Warning,' *American Political Science Review* **73**: 171-80.

CIA (1980), 'International Terrorism in 1979,' PA 80-100724, April, Washington, DC, National Foreign Assessment Center, Central Intelligence Agency.

Christensen-Szalanski, J. J. J. and J. B. Bushyhead (1981), 'Physicians' Use of Probabilistic Information in a Real Clinical Setting,' *Journal of Experimental Psychology*: Human Perceptions and Performance **7**: 928-35.

Colburn, F. D. (1982), 'Current Studies of Peasants and Rural Development: Applications of the Political Economy Approach,' *World Politics* **34** (April): 437-49.

Cooper, M. N. (1974), 'A Reinterpretation of the Causes of Turmoil: The Effects of Culture and Modernity,' *Comparative Political Studies* **7** (October): 267-91.

Crenshaw, M. (1981), 'The Causes of Terrorism,' *Comparative Politics* **13** (July): 379-99.

Cuzan, A. G. and R. J. Heggen (1982), 'Persuasion, Coercion and Scope: A Micro-Political Explanation of the 1979 Nicaraguan Revolution,' *Latin American Research Review* **17**: 156-70.

Dahlgren, H. E. (1976), 'Profile of Violence: An Analytical Model,' PR 76-10025, June, Washington, DC, Central Intelligence Agency.

Dahlgren, H. E. (1978), 'Operationalizing a Theoretical Model: Profiles of Violence in Argentina, Ethiopia, and Thailand,' pp. 59-103 in R. J. Heuer, Jr. (ed.), *Quantitative Approaches to Political Intelligence: The CIA Experience*, Boulder, CO, Westview.

Daly, J. and S. J. Andriole (1979), 'Problems of Quantitative Monitoring and Warning: Illustrations from the Middle East,' *Jerusalem Journal of International Relations* **4**: 31–74.

Davies, J. (1962), 'Toward a Theory of Revolution,' *American Sociological Review* **27** (February): 5–19.

Davies, J. (1969), 'The J-Curve of Rising and Declining Satisfactions as a Cause of Some Great Revolutions and a Contained Rebellion,' pp. 671–709 in H. D. Graham and T. R. Gurr (eds), *Violence in America: Historical and Comparative Perspectives*, New York, Signet.

Dibble, U. (1981), 'Socially Shared Deprivation and the Approval of Violence: Another Look at the Experience of American Blacks During the 1960s,' *Ethnicity* **8** (June): 149–68.

Disch, A. (1979), 'Peasants and Revolts,' *Theory and Society* **7** (March): 243–52.

Doran, C. (1978), 'U.S. Foreign Aid and The Unstable Polity: A Regional Case Study,' *Orbis* **22**: 435–52.

Duncan, G. T. and B. L. Job (1980), 'Probability Forecasting in International Affairs,' Final Report, April, Pittsburgh, PA, Carnegie-Mellon University.

Eckstein, H. (1980), 'The Approaches to Explaining Collective Political Violence,' pp. 135–66 in T. R. Gurr (ed.), *Handbook of Political Conflict*, New York, Free Press.

Einenstadt, S. (1978), *Revolution and the Transformation of Societies: A Comparative Study of Civilizations*, New York, Free Press.

Eisenstadt, S. (1980), 'Cultural Orientations, Institutional Entrepreneurs, and Social Change: A Comparative Analysis of Traditional Civilizations,' *American Journal of Sociology* **85** (January): 840–69.

Feierabend, I. K. and R. L. Feierabend (1966), 'Aggressive Behavior within Polities, 1948–1962: A Cross-National Study,' *Journal of Conflict Resolution* **10**: 249–71.

Feierabend, I. K. and R. L. Feierabend (1972), 'Systematic Conditions of Political Aggression: An Application of Frustration–Aggression Theory', in I. K. Feierabend, R. L. Feierabend, and T. R. Gurr (eds), *Anger, Violence, and Politics: Theories and Research*, Englewood Cliffs, NJ, Prentice-Hall.

Feierabend, I. K., R. L. Feierabend, and T. R. Gurr (eds) (1972), *Anger, Violence, and Politics: Theories and Research*, Englewood Cliffs, NJ, Prentice-Hall.

Fenmore, B. and T. J. Volgy (1978), 'Short-Term Economic Change and Political Instability in Latin America,' *Western Political Quarterly* **31** (December): 548–64.

Folger, R., D. Rosenfield, and T. Robinson (1983), 'Relative Deprivation and Procedural Justifications,' *Journal of Personality and Social Psychology* **45**: 268–73.

Gebelein, C. A., C.· E. Pearson, and M. Silbergh (1978), 'Assessing Political Risk of Oil Investment Ventures,' *Journal of Petroleum Technology* (May): 725-30.

Geller, D. S. (1982), 'Economic Modernization and Political Instability in Latin America: A Causal Analysis of Bureaucratic-Authoritarianism,' *Western Political Quarterly* 35 (March): 33-49.

George, A. L. (1979), 'Cast Studies and Theory Development: The Method of Structured, Focused Comparison,' pp. 43-68 in P. G. Lauren (ed.), *Diplomacy: New Approaches in History, Theory and Policy*, New York, Free Press.

Godson, R. (ed.) (1979), *Intelligence Requirements for the 1980s: Elements of Intelligence*, Washington, DC, National Strategy Information Centre.

Godson, R. (ed.) (1980), *Intelligence Requirements for the 1980s: Analysis and Estimates*, New Brunswick, NJ, Transaction Books.

Godson, R. and R. Shultz (1981-82), 'Foreign Intelligence: A Course Syllabus,' *International Studies Notes* 8: 4-16.

Goldstone, J. A. (1980), 'Theories of Revolution: The Third Generation,' *World Politics* 32 (April): 425-53.

Govea, R. M. and G. T. West (1981), 'Riot Contagion in Latin America 1949-1963,' *Journal of Conflict Resolution* 25 (June): 349-68.

Greene, T. H. (1974), *Comparative Revolutionary Movements*, Englewood Cliffs, NJ, Prentice-Hall.

Guimond, S. and L. Dubé-Simard (1983), 'Relative Deprivation Theory and the Quebec Nationalist Movement: The Cognition-Emotion Distinction and the Personal-Group Deprivation Issue,' *Journal of Personality and Social Psychology* 44: 526-35.

Gurr, T. R. (ed.) (1980), *Handbook of Political Conflict*, New York, Free Press.

Gurr, T. R. (1968a), 'A Causal Model of Civil Strife: A Comparative Analysis Using New Indices,' *American Political Science Review* 62 (December): 1104-24.

Gurr, T. R. (1968b), 'Psychological Factors in Civil Violence,' *World Politics* 20 (January): 245-78.

Gurr, T. R. (1970), *Why Men Rebel*, Princeton, NJ, Princeton University Press.

Gurr, T. R. (1974a), 'The Neo-Alexandrians: A Review Essay on Data Handbooks in Political Science,' *American Political Science Review* 68 (March): 243-52.

Gurr, T. R. (1974b), 'Persistence and Change in Political Systems, 1800-1971,' *American Political Science Review* 68 (December): 1482-504.

Gurr, T. R. (1979), 'Some Characteristics of Political Terrorism in the 1960s,' pp. 23-50 in M. Stohl (ed.), *The Politics of Terrorism*, New York, Marcel Dekker.

Gurr, T. R. and V. F. Bishop (1976), 'Violent Nations, and Others,' *Journal of Conflict Resolution* **20** (March): 80–110.

Gurr, T. R. and R. Duvall (1973), 'Civil Conflict in the 1960s: A Reciprocal Theoretical System with Parameter Estimates,' *Comparative Political Studies* **6** (July): 135–69.

Gurr, T. R. and M. I. Lichbach (1979), 'A Forecasting Model for Political Conflict Within Nations,' in J. D. Singer and M. D. Wallace (eds), *To Augur Well: Early Warning Indications in World Politics*, Beverly Hills, CA, Sage.

Haendal, D. (1979), *Foreign Investments and the Management of Political Risk*, Boulder, CO, Westview.

Haendel, D. (1981), 'Corporate Strategic Planning: The Political Dimension,' *The Washington Papers* **14**, 86, Beverly Hills, CA, Sage.

Halperin, M. and A. Kanter (eds) (1973), *Readings in American Foreign Policy: A Bureaucratic Perspective*, Boston, MA, Little, Brown.

Haner, F. T. (1975), 'Business Environment Risk Index,' *Best's Review*, Property/Liability Insurance Edition (July).

Hannan, M. T. and G. R. Carroll (1981), 'Dynamics of Formal Political Structure: An Event-History Analysis,' *American Sociological Review* **46** (February): 19–35.

Harmel, R. (1980), Gurr's "Persistence and Change" Revisited: Some Consequences of Using Different Operationalizations of "Change of Polity," ' *European Journal of Political Research* **8** (June): 189–214.

Hechter, M. (1975), *Internal Colonialism: The Celtic Fringe in British National Development, 1536-1966*, London, Routledge and Kegan Paul.

Heggen, R. J. and A. J. Cuzan (1981), 'Legitimacy, Coercion and Scope: An Expansion Path Analysis Applied to Five Central American Countries and Cuba,' *Behavioral Science* **26** (April): 143–52.

Helmer, O. (1978), 'The Use of Expert Opinions in International Relations Forecasting,' pp. 116-23 in N. Choucri and T. W. Robinson (eds), *Forecasting in International Relations: Theory, Method, Problems, Prospects*, San Francisco, CA, W. H. Freeman.

Heuer, R. J. (1981a), 'Strategic Deception and Counterdeception: A Cognitive Process Approach,' *International Studies Quarterly* **25** (June): 294–327.

Heuer, R. J. (1981b), 'Applications of Bayesian Inference in Political Intelligence,' in G. Hopple and J. Kulhman (eds), *Expert-Generated Data*, Boulder, CO, Westview.

Heuer, R. J. (ed.) (1978), *Quantitative Approaches to Political Intelligence: The CIA Experience*, Boulder, CO, Westview.

Hibbs, D. A., Jr (1973), *Mass Political Violence: A Cross-National Causal Analysis*, New York, John Wiley.

Himmelstein, J. L. and M. S. Kimmel (1981), 'States and Revolutions:

The Implications and Limits of Skocpol's Structural Model,' *American Journal of Sociology* **86** (March): 1145–54.

Hogarth, R. M. (1981), 'Beyond Discrete Biases: Functional and Dysfunctional Aspects of Judgmental Heuristics,' *Psychological Bulletin* **90**: 197–217.

Hopple, G. W. (1978), 'Final Report of the Cross-National Crisis Indications Project,' College Park, MD, University of Maryland.

Hopple, G. W. (1980a), 'Internal and External Crisis Early Warning and Monitoring,' *Interim Technical Report* TR 80-1-4, (December), McLean, VA, International Public Policy Research Corporation.

Hopple, G. W. (1980b), *Political Psychology and Biopolitics: Assessing and Predicting Elite Behavior in Foreign Policy Crises*, Boulder, CO, Westview.

Hopple, G. W. (1982a), 'International News Coverage in Two Elite Newspapers,' *Journal of Communication* **32** (Winter): 61–74.

Hopple, G. W. (1982b), 'Transnational Terrorism: Prospects for a Causal Modeling Approach,' *Terrorism* **6**: 73–100.

Hopple, G. W. and L. S. Falkowski (eds) (1982), *Political Psychology, Biopolitics, and International Politics*, New York and London, St. Martin's and Frances Pinter.

Hopple, G. W. and J. A. Kuhlman (eds) (1981), *Expert-Generated Data: Applications in International Affairs*, Boulder, CO, Westview.

Hopple, G. W. and P. J. Rossa (1981), 'International Crisis Analysis: Recent Developments and Future Directions,' pp. 65–97 in P. T. Hopmann, *et al.* (eds), *Cumulation in International Relations Research*, Denver, CO, University of Denver, Monograph Series in World Affairs.

Hopple, G. W., S. J. Andriole, and A. Freedy (eds) (1983), *National Security Crisis Forecasting and Management*, Boulder, CO, Westview.

Horowitz, D. (1982), 'Dual Authority Polities,' *Comparative Politics* **14** (April): 329–49.

Huntington, S. P. (1968), *Political Order in Changing Societies*, New Haven, CT, Yale.

Jackman, R. W. (1978), 'The Predictability of Coups d'Etat: A Model with African Data,' *American Political Science Review* **72** (December): 1262–75.

Jackman, R. W. and W. A. Boyd (1979), 'Multiple Sources in the Collection of Data in Political Conflict,' *American Journal of Political Science* **23** (May): 434–59.

Jacob, J. E. (1981), 'Ethnic Mobilization on the Germanic Periphery: The Case of the South Tyrol,' *Ethnic Groups* **3**: 253–80.

Jacobson, A. L. (1973a), 'Intrasocietal Conflict: A Preliminary Test of a Structural Level Theory,' *Comparative Political Studies* **6** (April): 62–83.

Jacobson, A. L. (1973b), 'Measuring Intrasocietal Conflict,' *Sociological Methods and Research* **4** (May): 440–61.

Johnson, C. (1964), *Revolution and the Social System*, Stanford, CA, Stanford University, The Hoover Institution on War, Revolution and Peace.

Johnson, C. (1966), *Revolutionary Change*, Boston, MA, Little, Brown.

Kaplan, A. (1964), *The Conduct of Inquiry*, Scranton, PA, Chandler Publishing.

Kerbo, H. R. (1978), 'Foreign Involvement in the Preconditions for Political Violence: The World System and the Case of Chile,' *Journal of Conflict Resolution* **23** (March): 41–69.

Kick, E. L. (1980), 'World Systems Properties and Mass Political Conflict Within Nations: Theoretical Framework,' *Journal of Political and Military Sociology* **8** (Fall): 175–90.

Kobrin, S. J., with J. Basek, S. Blank, and J. LaPalombara (1980), 'The Assessment and Evaluation of Non-Economic Environments by American Firms: A Preliminary Report', *Journal of International Business Studies* (Spring/Summer).

Korpi, W. (1974), 'Conflict, Power and Relative Deprivation,' *American Political Science Review* **68** (December): 1569–78.

Laemmle, P. (1977), 'Epidemiology of Domestic Military Intervention: Evaluation of Contagion as an Explanatory Concept,' *Behavioral Science* **22**: 327–33.

LaPalombara, J. (1982), 'Assessing the Political Environment for Business: A New Role for Political Scientists?', *PS* (Spring): 180–6.

Lasswell, H. D. (1936), *Politics: Who Gets What, When, How*, New York, McGraw-Hill.

LeBon, G. (1913), *The Psychology of Revolutions*, New York, Ernest Benn Limited.

Leifer, E. M. (1981), 'Competing Models of Political Mobilization: The Role of Ethnic Ties,' *American Journal of Sociology* **87**: 23–47.

Li, R. P. Y. and W. R. Thompson (1975), 'The "Coup Contagion" Hypothesis,' *Journal of Conflict Resolution* **19** (March): 63–88.

Lichbach, M. I. and T. R. Gurr (1981), 'The Conflict Process: A Formal Model,' *Journal of Conflict Resolution* **25** (March): 3–29.

Linehan, W. J. (1976), 'Models for the Measurement of Political Stability,' *Political Methodology*: 441–86.

Lipset, S. M. (1960), *Political Man: The Social Bases of Politics*, Garden City, NY, Doubleday.

Lupsha, P. A. (1971), 'Explanation of Political Violence: Some Psychological Theories Versus Indignation,' *Politics and Society* **3**: 89–104.

Maatsch, S. J., E. L. Johnson, G. W. Hopple, and M. A. Daniels (1980), 'Social Movements: Theories, Typologies, and Case-Studies,' *Technical Report* 80-C-3, October, McLean, VA, International Public Policy Research Corporation.

McCarthy, J. D. and M. N. Zald (1977), 'Resource Mobilization and Social

Movements: A Partial Theory,' *American Journal of Sociology* **82**: 1212–40.

McHale, V. E. (1978), 'Economic Development, Political Extremism and Crime in Italy,' *Western Political Quarterly* **31** (March): 59–79.

Mack, A. (1975), 'Numbers Are Not Enough: A Critique of Internal/ External Conflict Behavior Research,' *Comparative Politics* **7**: 597–618.

McPhail, C. (1971), 'Civil Disorder Participation: A Critical Examination of Recent Research,' *American Sociological Review* **36**: 1058–73.

Markides, K. C. and S. F. Cohen (1982), 'External Conflict/Internal Cohesion: A Reevaluation of an Old Theory,' *American Sociological Review* **47** (February): 880–98.

Merkl, P. H. (1981), 'Democratic Development, Breakdowns, and Fascism,' *World Politics* **34** (October): 114–35.

Merritt, R. (1971), *Systematic Approaches to Comparative Politics*, Chicago, IL, Rand McNally.

Mickolus, E. F. (1978), 'An Events Data Base for Analysis of Transnational Terrorism,' in R. J. Heuer, Jr. (ed.), *Quantitative Approaches to Political Intelligence: The CIA Experience*, Boulder, CO, Westview.

Midlarsky, M. I. (1970), 'Mathematical Models of Instability and a Theory of Diffusion,' *International Studies Quarterly* **14** (March): 60–84.

Midlarsky, M. I. (1978), 'Analyzing Diffusion and Contagion Effects: The Urban Disorders of the 1960s,' *American Political Science Review* **72**: 996–1008.

Midlarsky, M. I. (1982), 'Scarcity and Inequality: Prologue to the Onset of Mass Revolution,' *Journal of Conflict Resolution* **26** (March): 3–38.

Midlarsky, M. I., M. Crenshaw, and F. Yoshida (1980), 'Why Violence Spreads: The Contagion of International Terrorism,' *International Studies Quarterly* **24** (June): 269–98.

Migdal, J. S. (1974), *Peasants, Politics, and Revolution: Pressures Toward Political and Social Change in the Third World*, Princeton, NJ, Princeton University Press.

Milburn, T. W. (1972), 'The Management of Crises,' pp. 259–77 in C. F. Hermann (ed.), *International Crises: Insights from Behavioral Research*, New York, Free Press.

Moore, B. (1966), *Social Origins of Dictatorship and Democracy: Lord and Peasant in the Making of the Modern World*, Boston, MA, Beacon.

Moritz, F. (1978), 'Cross-Impact Analysis: Forecasting the Future of Rhodesia,' pp. 31–45 in R. J. Heuer, Jr. (ed.), *Quantitative Approaches to Political Intelligence: The CIA Experience*, Boulder, CO, Westview.

Morrison, D. G. and H. M. Stevenson (1971), 'Political Instability in Independent Black Africa: More Dimensions of Conflict Behavior Within Nations,' *Journal of Conflict Resolution* **15**: 347–68.

Morrison, D. G., R. C. Mitchell, J. N. Paden, and H. M. Stevenson (1972), *Black Africa: A Comparative Handbook*, New York, Free Press.

Muller, E. N. (1977), 'Mass Politics: Focus on Participation,' *American Behavioral Scientist* 21 (September/October): 63–86.

Muller, E. N. (1979), *Aggressive Political Participation*, Princeton, NJ, Princeton University Press.

Muller, E. N. (1980), 'The Psychology of Political Protest and Violence,' pp. 69–99 in T. R. Gurr (ed.), *Handbook of Political Conflict*, New York, Free Press.

Muller, E. N. (1982), 'An Explanatory Model for Differing Types of Participation,' *European Journal of Political Research* 10 (March): 1–16.

Muller, E. N. and T. O. Jukam (1983), 'Discontent and Aggressive Political Participation,' *British Journal of Political Science* 13 (April): 159–79.

Muller, E. N. and C. J. Williams (1980), 'Dynamics of Political Support-Alienation,' *Comparative Political Studies* 33: 33–59.

Muller, E. N., T. O. Jukam, and M. A. Seligson (1982), 'Diffuse Political Support and Antisystem Political Behavior: A Comparative Analysis,' *American Journal of Political Science* 26 (May): 240–64.

Nielsen, F. (1980), 'The Flemish Movement in Belgium After World War II: A Dynamic Analysis,' *American Sociological Review* 45 (February): 76–94.

Nielsson, G. P. (1980), 'Toward Systematic Comparative Analysis of Nation-Groups as a Unit of Analysis in the Study of Intra-State Political Integration and Inter-State Relations,' presented at the Annual Meeting of the International Studies Association, Los Angeles, CA (March).

O'Kane, R. H. T. (1981), 'A Probabilistic Approach to the Causes of Coups d'Etat,' *British Journal of Political Science* 11 (July): 287–308.

O'Kane, R. H. T. (1983), 'Towards an Examination of the General Causes of Coups d'Etat,' *European Journal of Political Reserarch* 11: 27–44.

Olson, M. (1963), 'Rapid Growth as a Destabilizing Force,' *Journal of Economic History* 23 (December): 529–52.

Orlansky, J. (1970), 'The State of Research on Internal War,' Research Papers P-565, August, Arlington, VA, Institute for Defense Analysis, Science and Technology Division.

Overholt, W. (1977), 'An Organizational Conflict Theory of Revolution,' *American Behavioral Scientist* 20: 493–520.

Paige, J. M. (1975), *Agrarian Revolution: Social Movements and Export Agriculture in the Underdeveloped World*, New York, Free Press.

Payne, S. (1971), 'Catalan and Basque Nationalism,' *Journal of Contemporary History* 6: 31–9.

Pitcher, B. L., R. L. Hamblin, and J. L. L. Miller (1978), 'The Diffusion of Collective Violence,' *American Sociological Review* 43 (February): 23–35.

Ragin, C. C. (1979), 'Ethnic Political Mobilization: The Welsh Case,' *American Sociological Review* 44 (August): 619–35.

Rastogi, P. N. (1977), 'Societal Development as the Quintessence of World Development,' pp. 339–77 in K. W. Deutsch, et al. (eds), *Problems of World Modeling: Political and Social Implications*, Cambridge, MA, Ballinger.

Reid, E. F. (1983), 'An Analysis of Terrorism Literature: A Bibliometric and Content Analytic Study' (doctoral dissertation, University of Southern California).

Rejai, M. (1980), 'Theory and Research in the Study of Revolutionary Personnel,' pp. 100–31 in T. R. Gurr (ed.), *Handbook of Political Conflict*, New York, Free Press.

Rhodebeck, L. A. (1981), 'Group Deprivation: An Alternative Model for Explaining Collective Political Action,' *Micropolitics* 1: 239–67.

Robinson, J. A. (1972), 'Crisis: An Appraisal of Concepts and Theories,' pp. 20–35 in C. F. Hermann (ed.), *International Crises: Insights from Behavioral Research*, New York, Free Press.

Roeder, P. G. (1982), 'Rational Revolution: Extensions of the "Bi-Product" Model of Revolutionary Involvement,' *Western Political Quarterly* 35 (March): 5–23.

Rowe, E. T. (1974), 'Aid and Coups d'Etat: Aspects of the Impact of American Military Assistance Programs in the Less Developed Countries,' *International Studies Quarterly* 18: 239–55.

Rummel, R. J. (1963), 'Dimensions of Conflict Behavior Within and Between Nations,' *General Systems Yearbook* 8: 1–50.

Russell, D. E. H. (1974), *Rebellion, Revolution, and Armed Force: A Comparative Study of Fifteen Countries with Special Emphasis on Cuba and South Africa*, New York, Academic Press.

Russett, B. M. (1964), 'Inequality and Instability: The Relation of Land Tenure to Politics,' *World Politics* 16: 442–54.

Sanders, D. (1978), 'Away From a General Model of Mass Political Violence: Evaluating Hibbs,' *Quality and Quantity* 12 (June): 103–29.

Sanders, D. (1981), *Patterns of Political Instability*, New York, St. Martin's Press.

Schwartz, D. C. (1968), 'Toward a New Knowledge Base for Military Development Operations During Insurgencies,' *Orbis* 12 (Spring): 73–86.

Schwartz, D. C. (1972), 'Political Alienation: The Psychology of Revolution's First Stage,' in I. K. Feierabend, R. L. Feierabend, and T. R. Gurr (eds), *Anger, Violence, and Politics: Theories and Research*, Englewood Cliffs, NJ, Prentice-Hall.

Scolnick, J. M., Jr. (1974), 'An Appraisal of Studies of the Linkage Between Domestic and International Conflict,' *Comparative Political Studies* 6 (January): 485–509.

Scott, J. C. (1977), 'Peasant Revolution: A Dismal Science,' review article, *Comparative Politics* 9 (January): 231–48.

Sheehan, J. J. (1980), 'Barrington Moore on Obedience and Revolt,' *Theory and Society* **9** (September): 723–34.

Sigelman, L. (1979), 'Understanding Political Instability: An Evaluation of the Mobilization-Institutionalization Approach,' *Comparative Political Studies* **12** (July): 205–28.

Sigelman, L. and S. Feldman (1983), 'Efficacy, Mistrust, and Political Mobilization: A Cross-National Analysis,' *Comparative Political Studies* **16** (April): 118–43.

Sigelman, L. and M. Simpson (1977), 'A Cross-National Test of the Linkage Between Economic Inequality and Political Violence,' *Journal of Conflict Resolution* **22** (March): 105–28.

Skocpol, T. (1979), *States and Social Revolutions: A Comparative Analysis of France, Russia, and China*, Cambridge, MA, Harvard University Press.

Skocpol, T. (1982), 'What Makes Peasants Revolutionary?', review article, *Comparative Politics* **14** (April): 351–75.

Skocpol, T. and M. Somers (1980), 'The Uses of Comparative History in Macrosocial Inquiry,' *Comparative Studies in Society and History* **22** (April): 174–97.

Slater, R. O. and L. Orloski (1978), 'Governmental Change Indicators,' Final Report M-13, September, Bethesda, MD, Analytical Support Center, Mathtech, Inc.

Snyder, D. (1978), 'Collective Violence: A Research Agenda and Some Strategic Considerations,' *Journal of Conflict Resolution* **22** (September): 499–534.

Somers, M. R. and W. L. Goldfrank (1979), 'The Limits of Agranomic Determinism: A Critique of Paige's *Agrarian Revolution*,' *Comparative Studies in Society and History* **21** (July): 443–58.

Sorokin, P. A. (1925), *The Sociology of Revolution*, Philadelphia, PA, Lippincott.

Spector, B. I., J. R. Brownell, Jr., M. D. Hayes, G. A. Keynon, and J. A. Moore (1975), 'Quantitative Indicators for Defense Analysis,' Final Report, June, Arlington, VA, CACI, Inc.

Stein, A. A. (1976), 'Conflict and Cohesion: A Review of the Literature,' *Journal of Conflict Resolution* **20**: 148–72.

Stohl, M. (1975), 'War and Domestic Political Violence: The Case of the United States 1890-1970,' *Journal of Conflict Resolution* **19** (September): 379–416.

Stohl, M. (1980), 'The Nexus of Civil and International Conflict,' pp. 297–330 in T. R. Gurr (ed.), *Handbook of Political Conflict*, New York, Free Press.

Tai, C., E. Peterson, and T. R. Gurr (1973), 'Internal Versus External Sources of Anti-Americanism,' *Journal of Conflict Resolution* **17**: 455–88.

Taylor, C. L. and D. A. Jodice (1980), 'New Data for Comparative Political

Analysis: The World Handbook of Political and Social Indicators III,' *Comparative Foreign Policy Notes* (Summer).

Thornton, T. P. (1964), 'Terrorism as a Weapon of Political Agitation,' pp. 71-99 in H. Eckstein (ed.), *Internal War: Problems and Approaches*, New York, Free Press.

Tilly, C. (1975), 'Revolutions and Collective Violence,' pp. 483-555 in F. Greenstein and N. Polsby (eds), *Handbook of Political Science*, III, Reading, MA, Addison-Wesley.

Tilly, C. (1978), *From Mobilization to Revolution*, Reading, MA, Addison-Wesley.

Tilly, C. (1983), 'Speaking Your Mind Without Elections, Surveys, or Social Movements,' *Public Opinion Quarterly* 47 (Winter): 461-78.

Trimberger, K. E. (1978), *Revolution From Above: Military Bureaucrats and Development in Japan, Turkey, Egypt, and Peru*, New Brunswick, NJ, Transaction Books.

Van Dyke, V. (1960), *Political Science: A Philosophical Analysis*, Stanford, CA, Stanford University Press.

Verba, S. (1971), 'Sequences and Development,' pp. 283-316 in L. Binder, et al., *Crises and Sequences in Political Development* VII, Princeton, NJ, Princeton University Press.

Weede, E. (1978), 'U.S. Support for Foreign Governments or Domestic Disorder and Imperial Intervention, 1958-1965,' *Comparative Political Studies* 10 (January): 497-527.

Weede, E. (1981), 'Income Inequality, Average Income, and Domestic Violence,' *Journal of Conflict Resolution* 25 (December): 639-54.

Welfling, M. B. (1975), 'Models, Measurement and Sources of Error: Civil Conflict in Black Africa,' *American Political Science Review* 64 (September): 871-88.

Wolf, E. (1969), *Peasant Wars of the Twentieth Century*, New York, Harper & Row.

Wolf, E. (1977), 'Why Cultivators Rebel,' *American Journal of Sociology* 83 (November): 742-50.

Zimmermann, E. (1979a), 'Crises and Crises Outcomes: Towards a New Synthetic Approach,' *European Journal of Political Research* 7 (March): 67-115.

Zimmermann, E. (1979b), 'Explaining Military Coups d'Etat: Towards the Development of a Complex Causal Model,' *Quality and Quantity* 13 (October): 431-41.

Zimmermann, E. (1979c), 'Toward a Causal Model of Military Coups d'Etat,' *Armed Forces and Society* 5 (Spring): 387-413.

Zimmermann, E. (1980), 'Macro-Comparative Research in Political Protest,' pp. 167-237 in T. R. Gurr (ed.), *Handbook of Political Conflict*, New York, Free Press.

Glossary

Analogy. A powerful tool for political instability problem-structuring involving the description and application of past analytical experiences for present problems. Any method or technique which structures the past for present or future benefit.

Approaches. Criteria for selecting the questions and data to be brought to bear to address a specific problem. Examples include historical approaches, economic approaches, and psychological approaches.

Bar chart. A graphical representation of frequencies displayed as rectangles on a graph.

Batch computing. Computer-based analysis via the submission of analytical 'jobs' for subsequent processing.

Bayesian analysis. The application of information processing techniques and methods based upon Bayes' theorem of conditional probabilities.

Bivariate analysis. The analysis of two variables to determine how they associate, interrelate, and/or co-vary.

'Bureaucratic politics.' The politics connected with maneuvering through environments defined according to formal and informal rules of behavior, frequently inhibited by role playing and the skillful manipulation of the rules.

Causal model. A representation of a set of interrelated variables which directly and indirectly impact upon a dependent variable. When mathematically defined, a causal model is often described as an econometric model.

Chi Square (χ^2). A statistical test for determining whether or not (and to what degree) an empirical relationship could be the result of chance. A 0.95 chi square would indicate that there was only a 5 percent chance that the observations had occurred by chance.

Classificatory schema. Lists of variables organized according to a set of characteristics which highlight the similarities and differences among the variables.

Collective Action (CA). Charles Tilly's notion of how interests, organization, mobilization, and opportunity combine to precipitate action.

Comparative methods. Those methods which focus upon the similarities and differences among the phenomena under investigation.

Computer-based problem-solving. Problem-solving via the application of analytical computer software either interactively or in batch.

Computerized information banks. Information banks, like the *New York Times* Information Bank and the Lockheed Dialog™ System, which satisfy on-demand requests via access through remote computer terminals.

Constraint analysis. The realistic examination of all of the constraints which will inhibit the analytical process, including the lack of expertise, data, methodological expertise, analytical approaches, time, or support.

Contingency tables. Simple data arrays in rows and columns.

Coordinate graph. A four quadrant scatter diagram for displaying the values of cases according to the high and low values of two variables.

Correlation. A statistical procedure for measuring the relationship between two or more variables.

Cost-benefit analysis. Resource allocation and evaluation based upon subjective and objective cost and benefit assessments.

Cross-impact methods. Prediction and forecasting methods which recognize and define the co-impact of events. Yield probabilities of events based upon probabilities of other events.

Data and information. Subjective and objective opinions and facts used to describe, explain, predict, prescribe, and evaluate.

Data reliability. The confidence one has in a given objective or subjective data set, given its known strengths and weaknesses.

Decision analysis. The application of a formal quantitative method for decomposing decision situations according to the costs, benefits, and likelihoods connected with various decision alternatives.

Decision models. Descriptive, explanatory, prescriptive, predictive or evaluative representations of the relationships among decision-making procedures and decision-makers.

Decision tree. Graphic representation of decision options, costs, and benefits, and the probabilities of key uncertainties permitting the evaluation of decision alternatives.

Deductive methods. Those methods which involve the extraction of knowledge from existing analytical premises.

Delphi methods. Forecasting procedures whereby experts express formal judgments and opinions about the likelihood of future events and/or conditions anonymously and in multiple rounds in response to the feedback gained from the prior round.

'Disciplined' approaches. Those analytical approaches which are categorizeable according to the academic disciplines from which they borrow, including economic approaches, psychological approaches, and historical approaches.

Econometric models. Complex representations of political instability via the development of multiple interrelated regression equations. Mathematically defined causal models.

Empirical data. Data and information which is extracted from empirical observations.

Epistemology. The sub-field of philosophy which focuses upon the origin, nature, methods, and limits of knowledge.

Dependent variables. The object or target of descriptive, explanatory, and predictive analyses. Defined, described, explained, and predicted according to measurable changes in the independent variable(s).

Description. The process by which events and conditions are profiled in order to determine similarities, differences, ranges, variations, and interrelationships.

Descriptive political instability research. Research that attempts to define the components of political instability, political instability itself, and the stages of revolution and internal political crisis.

'Expert' judgments. Judgments or opinions elicited from recognized experts and then brought to bear upon an analytical problem. On the opposite end of the epistemological continuum from quantitative empirical data or information.

Explanation. The process by which events and conditions, often expressed as variables, are linked to one another in measurable relationships whereby the changes in one set of variables can be related to changes in another set of variables.

Explanatory political instability research. Research that attempts to identify the factors that explain why instability occurs.

Extrapolative forecasting methods. Those methods which rely upon the persistence of data over time, the projection of trends, simulations, scenarios, moving averages, and exponential smoothing in order to predict or forecast events and/or conditions.

Frameworks. Devices which identify, arrange, and interrelate variables in a way which permits the development of analytical models and testable hypotheses of political instability.

Frequency distribution. The presentation of data according to a specific variable in a graph, table, or chart.

Functional approaches. Those analytical approaches which are categorizeable according to the functions they seek to describe, explain, predict, forecast, prescribe, or evaluate, such as legal approaches, communications approaches, and systems approaches.

Hierarchical inference structuring. A Bayesian subjective forecasting technique which requires the identification and hierarchical organization of the activities, indicators, and data likely to impact probabilistically upon a set of mutually exclusive hypotheses about the likelihood of political instability.

Hypothesis. An 'if . . . then' statement frequently used to structure problems, brainstorm, and determine how variables interrelate statistically.

Independent variable. A variable hypothesized as influential upon a dependent variable. When tested and found to have measurable impact upon a dependent variable it can be offered as descriptive, explanatory or predictive variable.

Inductive methods. Those methods which involve the extraction of knowledge from perceptions of reality.

Interactive computing. Immediate, 'on-line' analysis via computer programs designed to respond directly to their users.

Interval level data. Data having equal intervals, such as temperatures and speeds.

Linear relationships. Straight line relationships without exponents, where the value of the dependent variable (Y) is predictably and linearly related to the value of the independent variable (X).

Measures of central tendency. Several statistics which summarize 'center' data values, including the mean, median, and mode.

Measures of variability. Several statistics which summarize the variability of data around its 'middle' value, including the range and standard deviation.

Methods. The means by which data and information are organized and manipulated, in conjunction with analytical approaches, in order to 'solve' analytical problems.

Mini-Delphi methods. Abbreviated forecasting procedures for conducting face-to-face Delphi exercises. Implemented when time and money are in short supply.

Models. Representations of reality, described graphically or mathematically, but always incompletely.

Multi-attribute utility analysis. Analysis which permits the evaluation of decision options and entities according to multi-dimensional definition of 'value' or 'worth,' which always involves the identification of multiple evaluative criteria.

Multiple/comparative case study analysis. The analysis of several instances of political instability instead of one (single case study analysis) or many (cross-national analysis).

Multiple correlation and regression. A statistical technique which permits the analysis of more than two independent variables *vis-à-vis* a dependent variable.

Multivariate analysis. The analysis of more than two variables to describe, explain or predict phenomena.

'Natural history school.' A qualitative descriptive school of researchers who concentrate upon the minute details of specific episodes of political instability and revolution.

Nominal level data. Data categorizeable only by name, such as days of the week and months of the year.

Ordinal level data. Measurable data without equal intervals, such as student grades where the 500th student is by no means four times the worker the 125th student is.

Prediction and forecasting. The process by which future events and/or conditions are identified and assessed.

Prediction and forecasting goals. Short, medium, and long-range, negative and positive, objective and normative predictive-forecasting goals which, together with objects, define the boundaries of the predictive-forecasting problem.

Prediction and forecasting objects. Events or conditions which, along with the identification of goals, define the boundaries of the predictive-forecasting problem.

Predictive political instability research. Research that attempts to identify the factors which predict to instability, ideally ranked according to their predictive power.

Probability diagrams. Graphic representations of the events and/or conditions likely to affect the probability of a target event or condition. Yield quantitative probabilities from calculation of 'path' probabilities.

Problem structuring. All activity designed to profile the essence of a problem-solving situation frequently involving the use of analogy, analytical frameworks, models, and hypothesis formation.

Product moment correlation coefficients. The statistic which measures the strength of the relationship between interval level variables. The squared correlation coefficient (r^2) is the coefficient of determination which signifies the variance of one variable which is explained by the variance in the other.

Qualitative methods. Those methods which rely primarily upon the collection and manipulation of subjective or expert-generated data.

Quantitative methods. Those methods which rely primarily upon the collection and manipulation of quantitative empirical, or objective, data.

Rank-order displays. A graphical display of variables ranked from highest to lowest and interconnected according to how they interrelate.

Regression. A statistical technique for measuring and defining the relationship between two or more variables in predictive terms.

Requirements analysis. The application of a variety of techniques for determining the characteristics of the problem to be tackled. The techniques include the use of questionnaires, critical incident profiling, and fault trees.

Resource allocation. The process by which limited resources are allocated across specific functions, optimally against a set of priorities.

Scatterplot. A graphic representation of the frequencies on a standard graph displayed by dots within the vertical and horizontal axes.

Single case study analysis. The analysis of a single instance of political instability rather than several (comparative case study analysis) or many (cross-national analysis).

Spearman's Rho. An ordinal level statistical test for determining the extent of the relationship between two variables ranging from −1 to +1.

Spurious relationships. Relationships which may be highly associated but completely unrelated causally.

Standard deviation. The measure of dispersion around the mean (or average) value of a set of frequency data points which measures just how spread-out and consistent the data set is.

Statistical significance. The results of significance tests to determine the likelihood of empirical observations occurring by chance. Test results below 0.95 mean that we have less than enough confidence to declare the observations statistically significant. Some often-used significance tests include Chi Square (χ^2), F tests, Fisher exact tests, and D tests.

Subjective data. Data and information which is elicted from experts.

Support. Human, mechanical, and electronic problem-solving apparati necessary for efficient and successful problem-solving.

Talent. Problem-solving expertise comprised of skill, experience, attitude, education, and training.

Taxonomies. Classificatory devices for highlighting the similarities and differences among phenomena.

Theoretical case studies. Studies which look at one case (an incident, a country, a revolutionary leader, a revolution) in great detail, with a view to validating a set of theoretical notions about political instability.

Time. An analytical tool whose effect can be maximized by the elimination of time-wasting activity and development of systematic time-scheduling procedures.

Time planning. The allocation of time resources; systematic time-scheduling.

Typologies. Formal devices which classify phenomena according to characteristics which are exclusive to the type. Knowledge of the type in a typology permits the prediction of specific characteristics and vice versa.

Univariate analysis. The analysis of a single variable to determine how it deviates within itself.

Yule's Q. A statistical test which measures the degree and direction of bivariate (two variable) associations, ranging from −1 to +1.

Author Index

Subject Index